The Dreamer Awakes

Alice Kane

THE
DREAMER
AWAKES

Edited by

Sean Kane

BROADVIEW PRESS

1995

BROADVIEW PRESS
71 Princess Street
Peterborough, Ontario
Canada K9J 7H5

in the United States of America
3576 California Road
Orchard Park, NY 14127

Canadian Cataloguing in Publication Data

Kane, Alice, 1908–
The dreamer awakes

Includes bibliographical references.
ISBN 1-55111-045-8 (bound) ISBN 1-55111-047-4 (pbk.)
1. Tales. I. Title.
GR76.K35 1994   398.2   C94-932144-3

1 2 3 4 5 6 · 98 97 96 95

This book

is dedicated to

Ruth Stedman

with gratitude

Contents

CONTENTS

Wives and Husbands

Rebirth and Return

THE dreamer awakes,

The shadow goes by;
When I tell you a tale,
The tale is a lie.

But ponder it well,
Fair maiden, good youth:
The tale is a lie,
What it tells is the truth.

Introduction

by Robert Bringhurst

ONCE UPON A TIME there was a storyteller. People sometimes passed her in the street and sat beside her in the streetcar, thinking she was much like any other woman – and she was, but she was not. Even in between the stories, when she spoke the words *a piece of bread* or the words *a glass of water*, she restored to these essentials all the dignity and magic they possessed before the clocks began to tick or money to be minted or food to come from stores. She undid an evil spell with nothing more than words. And yet it wasn't just the words, for they were often words that other people used. It was the way in which she said them. And the way she said them came from what she saw.

Once, long ago, she said – and half an hour later, with her crisp, methodical and nondramatic voice, full of little rising tones, like lapping water, she had washed, set and bandaged the entire broken world. Under the care of that voice, if we did not keep breaking the world again, it would be well and truly healed.

That time is now; that storyteller's name is Alice Kane. She was born into a world – the north of Ireland in 1908 – where a rich and complex oral literature persisted, side by side with a long tradition of writing. Most of the stories she tells now are stories she has read in books, but it was not from books she learned to tell them. In an oral culture, a story is heard, and in some of those who hear it, it becomes a vision. Those of its hearers who learn to *see* the story can tell it later themselves. Those who do not may learn to summarize or even to recite it, but that is not the same as *telling*. Alice Kane sees what she tells and tells what she sees. Often she has got not only images, events and names of characters but also turns of phrase from a book; nevertheless, she tells the story instead of reciting the text. She may tell the same tale dozens of times, and may insist that she is telling it the same way, in the same words, every time – yet each telling is different, because each telling grows afresh from the vision.

Her performances, in fact, are like those of many a great musician. They are neither, in the strict sense, *recitals* (playing note-for-note from the score or from memorization) nor pure *improvisations*, but re-creations, re-envisionings. And the stories, as they emerge from her, are thought-music. Their harmonies, cadences and rhythms are those of a great interpreter in touch with a great tradition.

That is the way real bread is baked, the way real water is caught from the spring. No two loaves and no two cups are quite the same.

Books and tapes are also not the same as live performance. In this book, transcribed from her performances, the vision is at rest and the text momentarily fixed – waiting to be read by someone else in whom again it will be kindled into vision.

That will happen. Stories find the tellers they need. They nest in us as saw-whet owls and wood ducks nest in trees. More than that, they use us to reproduce themselves. That is one of the parts – one of the few useful parts – humans appear to play in the global ecology.

Still, I am amazed by the way stories and songs, and the words of which they are made, preserve their forms over hundreds of years and thousands of miles, just as animals and plants do over many generations. Stories are not *copied*; they are *reborn*, and each succeeding individual is different, yet the species, for long stretches, is substantively the same. Even long and complex stories propagate themselves, not because of but primarily *in spite of* writing. Not the least of Alice Kane's accomplishments is her definitive demonstration that writing can, after all, be made to serve instead of displace the oral tradition.

A book, like a bellows or a bicycle, is a simple kind of machine, for which the reader provides the motive power. At its best, a book is a fluent, organic machine, made from plant fibre, vegetable oils and carbon, and from the delicate bones of letters, carved in two dimensions by microscopic motions of the hand. Even the best-made book is nevertheless like the bicycle, not like the body: the book is not alive. It may still be useful to the story – as a dead tree can be useful to flickers and sapsuckers: as a place to nest and feed – but until the bird comes to the tree, or the reader who is a visionary listener comes to the book, nothing can happen.

The book is different, though, from the radio, television and film, just as the bicycle is from cars and trucks and trains. These machines have engines of their own and predetermined paths. Automobiles and trains have abbreviated, standardized and brutalized many people's journeys. Radio and television have had the same effect on many people's stories, and schools the same effect upon their minds. Alice Kane's achievement and her legacy are the greater because she has practised her art with steadiness and grace in a difficult time. She has made herself an elder of the tribeless as well as of the tribe.

Stories nourish and preserve themselves through artists such as she. In doing so, they preserve, over long distances, detailed patterns of meaning. They preserve the names and genealogies of the gods, the geography of neolithic villages, the courtesies and gestures of old times, and the patterns formed by the paths between the worlds. The paths, for instance, between the world of the village and the world of the forest; between childhood and marriage, community and solitude, and the paths between the worlds of life and death, and the worlds of waking and dream.

We have many names for different kinds of stories, but all such terms are vague, except to critics who make them brittle. If the story is textured or structured in some seemingly inexhaustible way, we are apt to call it a poem. If it forms a long chain of adventurous episodes, we may call it a saga or even an epic. If it lays a heroic or totemic foundation for history, we will probably call it a legend. If it maps the structure of the cosmos – even some small corner of the cosmos – we are likely to call it a myth. If it commingles gods and humans with the emphasis on the gods, we are likely, again, to call it myth. If it mingles gods and humans with emphasis on the humans, or turns the human world over like a stone to show its hidden, magical side, we may call it a *wondertale*.

Tales of that kind – which are found in oral traditions around the world – are Alice Kane's particular specialty. The genre is highly developed in the oral literatures of Russia and of Ireland; and these are the two traditions on which Alice Kane has drawn most heavily. But the wondertale is highly developed in many Native American, Asian and Oceanic oral literatures as well. Its roots lie deep in the paleolithic, yet it can thrive in the dilapidated sideyards and margins of great empires, where aristocrats and peasants, with their two very different kinds of poverty and wealth, stand at the edge of human intervention, facing the persistent rich enigma of the world.

The thick compendia of modern literary scholarship – the *Princeton Encyclopedia of Poetry and Poetics*, for example – have nothing to say about wonder, though they have much to say about satire, irony, wit, and the more superficial features of versification. But wonder lies at the heart of poetry. Without it, wit is empty, and all the fancy stitchery of metre, rhyme and assonance is sham. Alice Kane breaks into verse now and again in some of her stories, but the *poetry* in the stories is in the wonder at their centres and in the thought-music that shapes them from end to end.

The heroes of wondertales, more often than not, are unlikely creatures, open to wonder themselves. They are Davids, not Goliaths. If they are well-born, they will probably lose every advantage of wealth and position before gaining what they seek. If the winning comes more easily than that, they will probably lose what they gain. But most importantly, I think, a wondertale opens doors or windows between the worlds.

One of these worlds, mentioned often in this book, is the world of Faërie. Writers as early as Shelley, at the beginning of the 19th century, felt it useful to write the name this way, with a diaeresis over the E, to remind their readers and themselves not to lose the middle syllable. It is pronounced as the Tudor writers often spelled it: *fayerie*. Faërie is the country of the fays, who are called, in another dialect of English, fairies. But it is home to many more creatures than that. It is the Otherworld – or one of the other worlds – adjacent to and parallel with this one: the world beyond the daylight and the road, beyond the furrow and the fence, outside the reach of parliaments and church bells, where human institutions are not in control. In North America, we call this world Nature or the Wild.

If *Faërie* and *fairy* seem fragile and quaint words by comparison, it is worth our while to look at them more closely. Some scholars derive them from the Latin *fari* and Greek φημί, to speak. But the real etymology is different. Homer, Pindar and other early poets call the satyrs and centaurs φῆρεϛ (*phêres*). The singular is φήρ.[1] This word is applied to things that hunt and are hunted; it means *creatures of the wild*. It is sister to the Latin *ferus*, whose descendants in English include the words *feral, ferocious* and *fierce*. Faërie is, or was once, not a playground filled with diminutive amusements for young minds but the myth-world itself, which is everything outside of our control. Faërie is an old name for the world of nonhumans that surrounds, feeds and (sometimes) tolerates us all.

One value of the wondertale, then, is that it confirms a relationship between human beings and gods. Not gangs or tribes of humans, and not God the all-knowing and all-powerful, but individual humans and individual gods. The wondertale is polytheistic and pagan, no matter how many Jewish, Christian or Muslim trappings it may bear. Its gods are close at hand and have limited powers. Its human protagonists lack the well-aged, battle-tested guile of Odysseus or the stature of Achilles, and they have no troops or ships at their command.

The stakes are always high in a wondertale – life or death, or a lifetime of fortune versus failure, or good marriage versus bad – and there is typically a strong tide, a breathtaking movement back and forth between this world and the other, and down and up (or up and down) the scale. This makes hearing a wondertale, or telling one, exciting – like taking a kayak out through the surf, or like rounding a point in a small boat, com-

---

1 In the dialect of Athens, the form was θήρ, which survives in words like *theriomorphic* and in the German word for wild animal, *Tier*.

ing out of sheltered water into the big swells. A wondertale takes us through the mountains of the spirit, crossing a high pass. It is also an education in how to live right here and now. The inhabitants of Faërie are or represent real things. Meeting them abruptly in the stories is like coming suddenly into the midst of a school of dolphins or a pod of killer whales. In a real story, we meet them alone, on their terms and their turf, not being put through their paces by trainers, in front of screaming crowds, in aquarium pools.

So the world of the wondertale is close to the world of the vision quest. It is a world where humans find and stretch their limits, establish their interdependence with their nonhuman neighbours, and make themselves at home within a universe they do not, cannot, need not, must not fully understand.

The wondertale can do much else as well, of course, when pressure is brought to bear. It can serve as a witty mirror of human society, and it can crackle with literary style and conceit. Wondertales of that sort were in fashion in Paris salons at the end of the 17th century. These were written to be read, not told, to audiences able to appreciate their topical and literary allusions, satiric portraits and sly barbs. The movement was begun, it seems, by Charles Perrault, to whom we owe the first literary versions of the Mother Goose stories, and it was brought to a kind of premature fruition by Marie-Catherine d'Aulnoy. But at that end of the spectrum, the wondertale has left the world of myth and needs another name. Its subject is not the relation of humans to gods but the relation of humans to humans – though fairies, cats and witches may be made to serve a catalytic role. And fairy tale, not wondertale, appears to be the name d'Aulnoy and her colleagues themselves preferred.

Alice Kane is well acquainted with tales of this kind too. But her own work as a storyteller has led her up the path in the opposite direction — toward the timeless, toward the archetype, and far away from topical concerns. D'Aulnoy's stories, written with immense skill, are centred on the audience they seek, and on that audience's sense of privileged insight into worldly affairs. The telling of myth is centred on the myth, and on the subject of the myth, which is the deep, recurrent world. The myth is told in order to draw its listeners back into contact with that world and out of the trap of daily concerns and current affairs. Sean Kane, a teacher and a scholar of the first rank, who has listened longer and more deeply than anyone else to the stories his aunt Alice has told for sixty years, says what he hears in her voice is "the music of humanity at peace with time, and with the earth, and with mortality."

Time, the earth and death are living things, as stories are — so long as other living things exist to feed them, and for them to nourish in their turn.

Bowen Island, British Columbia
February 1995

To Seek a Fortune

Ivon Tortik

H E WAS BORN on the coast of
Brittany, where God's sea is vast but the fish are small, and
when his mother took him to the church to be christened, she
tied a piece of black bread around his neck to show, she said,
that he'd always be poor, and he'd always be ugly. But she was
wrong, as we will see.

Poor he certainly was. His father was Perik the fisherman,
and when he had a good catch he drank it all away at the wine
shop. When he had a poor catch there was nothing to eat in the
house.

Ugly he was too. Oh, he was ugly! He had a hump on his
back as big as the priest's belly. He had little spindly legs, eyes
dull and flat as pebbles, skin of no colour, hair of no colour.
All the little boys ran after him as he walked down the road
crying, "Ivon Tortik, Ivon Tortik," which means Ivon the
humpback.

You know, he didn't care. He didn't care at all. He was perfectly happy. If there was no food in the house he ate berries
from the hedges, and roots, and things that he could find. And
he loved Brittany.

He loved to draw. He would draw with a wet finger on any dry surface. He would draw with his finger in the sand: ships, flowers, stars, trees, girls' faces — all of these he loved. One day he found an old broken penknife with one rusty blade left. And now he could cut pictures into trees, even occasionally into rocks. Wherever he went he made pictures.

He was perfectly happy — until the day that he met Margaridde, the Pleumeur miller's daughter. She was the most beautiful girl in all Brittany. Her cheeks were pink like the little roses in the hedges. Her eyes were blue like the Breton sky. Her hair was golden like the broom, and not only was she the most beautiful girl in all of Brittany, she was also the richest. Her father, the Pleumeur miller, owned more than half the orchards and nearly all of the mills in the province. And Ivon Tortik took one astonished look at her and turned and ran home as fast as he could go. He washed his face and brushed his hair and put on his father's wooden shoes that he wore to church on Sundays. And he put on his father's Sunday hat. And he shambled back to the home of Margaridde. She was sitting out on her balcony, spinning. And suddenly he stood there in front of the steps, and he looked up at her, and he said, "Margaridde, Pleumeur miller's daughter, I want to marry you. I want to eat out of the same fork and drink out of the same cup all of the days of our lives."

And she looked at him standing there: poor, ugly, crooked — and she laughed. And her laughter was like the pearls from a string as they break and fall one by one to the ground. And she said, "All right, Ivon Tortik, I'll marry you. I'll marry you when you are as straight as the poplar trees on the Kergrist road, and when there are more gold pieces in your pockets than there are apples on my father's apple trees."

"All right," he said. "All right, Margaridde. Don't you marry anyone else while I'm gone."

And he set off down the road to find himself a straight back and a pocketful of gold.

It was a long time before he found them. He walked and walked. But one night – one autumn night – he came to a little village on the edge of a moor, and it was All Hallows' Eve. The people in the village said to him, "Keep away from the moor tonight. It's All Hallows' night, and the fairies dance. They'll do you some harm if they find you there on the moor."

"Harm?" thought Ivon Tortik. "What harm could anyone do to me? What could anyone do to me? They couldn't make me uglier, they couldn't make me poorer; besides, I'd like to see the fairies dance." So he went out and lay at the edge of the moor, dozed away the afternoon, the early evening – and then, he suddenly felt the ground begin to shake under his feet, and it was midnight, and the little people had come out to dance.

They were small, small as your thumb. White as paper their faces were. And their hair and eyes black as ink. They took hands in one great circle that went all the way round the moor. But there were thousands of them. And they danced – round and round they danced. And they sang, as they danced, one monotonous song that went:

> *Monday, Tuesday;*
> *Monday, Tuesday;*
> *Monday, Tuesday and Wednesday.*
>
> *Monday, Tuesday;*
> *Monday, Tuesday;*
> *Monday, Tuesday and Wednesday.*

Ivon Tortik pulled himself up on his elbows to see better. He pulled himself a little higher, and still the dance went on and still the song went on:

> Monday, Tuesday;
> Monday, Tuesday;
> Monday, Tuesday and Wednesday.

> Monday, Tuesday;
> Monday, Tuesday;
> Monday, Tuesday and Wednesday.

Suddenly the dancers stopped. And a voice cried, "Look, look, Ivon Tortik is watching us. Come on, Ivon Tortik, come and dance."

"I can't dance," he said. "I can't dance. Can't you see that I can't dance? I'm a cripple."

"Come," they said, "dance with us. If you watch, you must dance." And they dragged him into the dance. And there he was, going round and round with the rest, one foot up and one foot down, round and round in a circle, and still the song went on:

> Monday, Tuesday;
> Monday, Tuesday . . .

He thought he couldn't lift his foot again. He was dizzy, he was tired, he was exhausted. And at last he called out in the loudest voice he could, "Stop it! Stop that silly song!"

They stopped. "Silly song?" they said. "Silly song? What do you mean silly song? It's an old, old song. It's the oldest song in the world. Our grandfathers taught it to us, their grandfathers taught it to them. It's an old, old song."

"Well," he said, "there's nothing *wrong* with it. It's just that you only know half of it."

"You mean there's more?"

"Of course there's more," he said.

"Teach us the rest," they told him. "Teach us the rest. Come, let's dance." So they took hands and the circle began to move again, and the song went on:

> *Monday, Tuesday;*
> *Monday, Tuesday;*
> *Monday, Tuesday and Wednesday.*

And Ivon Tortik sang:

> *Thursday, Friday;*
> *Thursday, Friday;*
> *Thursday, Friday and Saturday.*
>
> *Thursday, Friday;*
> *Thursday, Friday;*
> *Thursday, Friday and Saturday.*

"Oh," they said, "Ivon Tortik, Ivon Tortik. You've taught us a new verse to our ancient song. How shall we reward you? Tell us Ivon Tortik. Would you rather be handsome, or would you rather be rich?"

Well, Ivon Tortik didn't know much. But one thing he did know was that fairy gold melts away in the pockets of mortal men. So he said, "I'll be handsome."

And do you know what they did? They picked him up, those little men – no bigger than your thumb, but there were thousands of them – they picked him up, and they threw him, up, up, up, into the air, till the cool clouds brushed against his hot forehead. And he fell to the ground with a great thud, and he remembered no more.

When he wakened, it was morning, bright morning. And he felt as if he really had been dancing all night. Every bone in his body ached. He was stiff, he was tired, and he was thirsty. He pulled himself to his feet, thinking, "What a dream that was!"

And he went down to a stream at the edge of the moor to get a drink. But as he bent over the water, he couldn't believe his eyes. For there reflected in the water was not his own colourless face, but a face brown as a berry, with bright-dark eyes, and hair black as the crow's wing. Trembling, and almost afraid to look, he pulled himself to his feet and stared at the reflection of his body in the water. His back was as straight as the poplar trees on the Kergrist road! Right there on the edge of that stream he danced a little dance. And he called, "Margaridde, miller's daughter, one half of you is mine!" And he started off down the road to look for pocketfuls of gold.

All November he walked, and well into December, and on Christmas Eve he found himself in another village at the edge of a moor. The villagers were very busy. They were getting ready. Full of Christmas preparations, they were, cooking and baking and cleaning and scrubbing. Everyone had something they had to do, and no one paid any attention at all to the stranger.

He wandered out onto the moor, and this moor had twelve standing stones on it – the great stones that stand on many ancient moors, in Brittany and other places. There were twelve of them, and they stood up like giants. Ivon Tortik picked the biggest one, and he sat down with his back against it. It was good to lean on. He sat there most of the evening, and thought his own thoughts, and suddenly he heard two crows talking to each other on top of the stone. You know that on Christmas

Eve all the creatures can talk? And the first crow said, "Look down there – that's Ivon Tortik, the humpback from the Pleumeur miller's village. But look, he's got himself a straight back and a handsome face from the fairies of the Pleubian moor. Now he's looking for pocketfuls of gold. He'll go a long way before he'll find those."

And the second one said, "A long way? Why, he's sitting on gold right now."

"What do you mean?" asked the first crow.

"Don't you know?" said the second. "All those great stones stand in pits of gold pieces from a long, long way back, a way back in history. But nobody could get at them, except that on Christmas Eve, while the church bells are ringing midnight, the stones go down to the river to drink their one drink of the year. When the first bell rings, they leave their holes, and they stalk down to the stream to drink, and then they come back again. And while they're gone, if he could leap into the hole, he could fill his pockets with gold in no time at all. But, he'd better be out of the hole before they fall into it again, because he'd be crushed to death."

"Oh, I never knew that," said the first crow. And then, chattering, they flew away.

And Ivon Tortik thought, "Well, I'll certainly stay here and see." So he stayed there.

All evening long he leaned against the stone. Then, because he had nothing else to do, he pulled his knife out of his pocket and began to make pictures in the stone: flowers, trees, fish, ships, girls' faces, and anything else that you could think of to draw, he drew. And then, because it was Christmas Eve, he cut a star into the rock. He cut it very, very deep. The edges were sharp. A Christmas star. And suddenly, he dozed off and forgot everything until the church bells began to ring for midnight.

They rang out, one great ring, and he felt the stone, against which he was leaning, shiver and pull itself up out of the ground. It got up and moved away, and all the other stones started to stalk like great, stiff giants down to the river to drink.

Two, rang the bells, and Ivon Tortik was in the pit that the stone had left.

Three — he was up to his waist in gold. He was filling his pockets, he was filling his sleeves, he was filling his great, wide hat with gold.

Four, five, six, seven, eight, nine, ten, eleven — Ivon Tortik looked up, and there, towering above him, was the stone about to slide back into its place. This was the end. There would be no time to scramble out, and in his mind he called "goodbye." Goodbye to Margaridde, goodbye to the Brittany that he loved, goodbye to the whole world. And then — and then a miracle happened, a real miracle. You remember, this was Christmas Eve, and the Christmas star was shining bright in the sky? And Ivon Tortik had carved a star, deep, deep into the rock? The Christmas star shone against the edge of it, and the light was so blinding that the great stone couldn't see its place, and instead of falling into its own hole, it fell over on its side. If you don't believe me, you can go to see it. It's there to this day — eleven of the stones standing straight and tall, and the twelfth one, with Ivon Tortik's carvings on it, lying on its side.

He didn't wait to examine anything. He pulled himself up as best he could out of the hole, his sleeves, his trouser legs, every-thing stiff with gold, and he started with his shambling walk as fast as he could towards Margaridde, the miller's daughter.

Christmas morning was bright and sunny. And Margaridde, the miller's daughter, went to Mass. And then she came home and sat in the sunshine on her balcony. She saw the strangest figure coming down the road. He walked so stiffly you'd have thought he was made of wood. He stopped at the foot of her steps, and he looked up at her, and he said, "Margaridde, did you marry anyone while I was gone?"

"Who are you?" she said. "Who are you?"

"I'm Ivon. Ivon that they used to call Ivon Tortik. But look, I got myself a straight back, straight as the poplar trees on the Kergrist road. And as for gold pieces..." He emptied out his pockets and his sleeves and his hat, and the gold pieces were thick upon the road.

"Margaridde," he said, "will you marry me?"

Yes, of course she would. She married him right there on Christmas Day in the morning. And they ate out of the same fork, and they drank out of the same cup, all the days of their lives.

The Tale of the Tsar Saltan and Prince Guidon

THREE MAIDS SAT DOWN to their spinning, and darkness came down all over the land. And the first maiden said, "If the Tsar were to marry me, I'd bake him pirozhki as sweet as the honey that the black bees cull."

And the second one said, "If the Tsar were to marry me, I would weave him sheets for his bed as soft as the breath of the summer breeze."

But the youngest one said, "If the Tsar were to marry me, I would bear him a son; and the mark of the Lord would be on him; and he would be an arshin long from head to foot; and he would be a mighty warrior and a wise ruler, yea, greater even than his father."

The Tsar was listening outside, and he smiled to himself. He came into the house and he lifted his hand and he said, "Peace to all here." And they all fell on their knees before him. But he lifted the youngest one up and he said, "Will you marry me, and come home to my palace with me, and bear me the son you just spoke of?"

And when she said she would, he said, "And your sisters can come with us. The first one can be mistress of my kitchens, and the second one can be in charge of my looms. And you will all have all you want."

So he led them home. As soon as they got to the palace they started the preparations for the wedding, because the whim of a Tsar is soon performed. And a great feast they had, and all the nobles and the rich people of the land came to the wedding. And after they had feasted, they led their Tsar and his new bride to a couch of ivory, and they wished them happiness and great joy in their marriage. Then everyone went to sleep, except the two sisters. And the one in the kitchen sat by the fire and wept. And the other one sat by her looms and wept. And they were filled with envy of their sister.

Then war came in a distant country, and the Tsar bade his wife farewell and told her to take care of herself — to be very careful of herself while he rode away to war — and he would come back as soon as he could.

And he rode off to the war. But he was gone for weeks and weary months. And in the middle of those weeks and weary months, she bore him a child. She bore him the son that she'd promised him. He was an arshin long from head to foot. He had the mark of the Lord upon him. And he looked wise and strong.

She was pleased and happy, and she wrote a letter and sent it by a messenger to her husband to tell him what had happened. But the sisters lay in wait for the messenger. They brought him in, and while he didn't know what was happening they took the letter from him and they put another letter in its place. And in it they wrote: "Lord Tsar, in the night your wife has borne you a son. It is neither male nor female. It is neither green frog nor grey mouse. It is some dark creature of the night."

When the Tsar got the letter he was distressed beyond belief. And he wept, and he was angry. And then he thought, "No. She is my wife. And I loved her." So he wrote and said, "Let no harm come to the Tsaritsa until I come home again. Take care of her. Guard her and the child well." And he gave the letter to the messenger and sent him home.

The sisters watched for him. They waylaid him again. They brought him into their house. They gave him glass after glass of red wine until he didn't know whether it was day or night, until he didn't know the hairs of his head from the fingers of his hand. And while he was sleeping the whole night long, they wrote another letter, and it said: "My boyars, my wise men, when you get this letter, take my wife and take my child and put them into a chest; and caulk all the seams with resin; and throw it into the sea."

And in the morning, when the messenger wakened up, they gave him the letter and they sent him home. When the boyars got the letter, they were very unhappy. They didn't know what to do. And they said, "She has done no harm. We won't kill her." So they went to her and they said, "We won't kill you, we won't put you in the chest. We will let you go, as long as you will go away and let no sight of you be here when the Tsar comes back."

But she said, "No. You would risk your lives to do that for me. Besides," she said, "I would prefer death, to life under my husband's displeasure."

So she dressed herself in her white dress. She washed her face and combed her hair. She bowed to a holy icon of the Lord. She took her baby in her hands, and she came down to the seashore. And the boyars, weeping, put her into the chest. And they caulked the seams with resin. And they threw it out into the blue sea-ocean. And she wept.

As for the baby, he grew. He didn't grow by the day or by the week — he grew by the minute and the hour. He grew strong and big and he said to her, "Mother, mother, what is the matter?" And she cried.

And he said, "Blue wave! Blue wave on which we are tossing, you are free, you can go wherever you like and play with your merry companions here, there, anywhere you want, while my mother, who has done no wrong, and I, a newborn babe, are shut up in this chest. Please, please, cast us up on a pleasant shore so that we won't perish in the waves."

And the little wave heard him, and tossed them up on a pleasant shore in the middle of the blue sea-ocean. But they were still in the chest, and the mother wept and wept.

But the child said to her, "Mother, cease your weeping. Look how I grow! Look how I grow! Soon I will get us out of this chest." And he pressed his feet on one end of it, and he pushed with his hands on the other end of it. And he was so strong, a real hero, and he pushed so hard that the chest split in two. And there they were, free, on an island, in the middle of the blue sea.

There was a hill in the middle of the island, and on the hill there grew an oak tree. And the boy was happy — he was very happy. But his mother went on weeping.

"Mother," he said, "stop weeping. Look, if you have food you will be better."

So he looked around, and he found what he needed and he made himself an arrow and a bow. He said goodbye to his mother and he went around to the other side of the island to see if he could find something for her to eat. And just as he got to the shore around on the other side of the island, he heard a cry, the cry of a bird, and he looked up and there was a great, black hawk and it had caught a swan. And though the swan beat her wings against the hawk as hard as she could, she was powerless against him.

The boy lifted his bow, and let his arrow speed, right through the heart of the hawk. The hawk gave a cry that was not the cry of a hawk, and it fell into the sea, and waters closed over it. But the swan – the swan brushed the water from her wings and she came up to the boy, and she said to him – in Russian – she said to him, "Think not that I am a swan, as I look to be, or that that was a hawk. For I am a princess and that was a sorcerer who has me under enchantment. But now you have killed him. And don't weep. Don't weep because you have wasted the arrow with which you thought to bring your mother food. Wait till morning, and I will repay the debt I owe. Sleep."

So he went back to his mother and he comforted her and told her to sleep; and they both slept well on the shore, all through the starry night. And when the morning dawned, they looked up and there on the hill above their heads was a great city – a city with turrets, spires, castles, palaces, soldiers, people coming, people going. The boy took his mother by the hand and they started up the hill. And the gates of the city were flung open, and the people in their bright clothes, chanting and singing, came out to meet them.

And they said, "You are our king, Guidon, you are our king! Come into your city, for it is yours."

And he said, "Mother, come with me into our city." And they lived there very, very happily.

Then one day some ships were washed up on their shore, and Guidon ran down to meet them. He brought the sailors ashore and he took them in and spread a great feast for them, and he said, "Who are you and where do you come from?"

They said, "We're ships from the Tsar Saltan, and we've

been across on the other side of the world gathering furs from the strange beasts for him, and now we are on our way home."

"Well," he said, "eat your fill and go your way; but tell the Tsar Saltan about my city, and that he should come and see me here. Tell him that Prince Guidon sends his greetings."

So they left. But as they left he stood on the shore and watched them go, and the tears ran down his face. And there before him was the swan, and she said to him, "Why do you cry, Guidon? Do you not have everything you want?"

And he said, "I cry because they go to my father's house, and I don't know my father, and I would like to follow these ships."

"Well," she said, "you can go after them." And she beat her wings and suddenly he was encompassed in a great mist. And when the mist died away he was a little gnat.

And she said, "Fly, fly out!"

So he flew after the ships until he came to the other side of the world, to the Tsar Saltan's kingdom, and he went ashore with the sailors and up to the palace. He went into the room where the Tsar Saltan sat. The Tsar sat on a throne. His face was dark and unhappy. And on either side of him sat his wife's two sisters.

He said to the sailors, "Greetings! Where have you been? Tell me what you have seen."

The sailors said, "We've been on the other side of the world; and on an island where there was nothing before but one oak tree, there's now a city with palaces and turrets and spires and armies and people. And the prince of the city said, "Give the Tsar Saltan greetings from Prince Guidon and tell him to come and visit me."

"Oh indeed, indeed I will go!" said the Tsar, and he looked happy for the first time in many days.

But the eldest sister said, "A city on an island in the middle of the sea! A tale for ignorant sailors! You don't want to go see that. Now *I* have seen a wonder worthy of a Tsar. I have seen a little squirrel that sits and cracks nuts. And those nuts he cracks have shells of gold, but the kernels are emeralds. And he piles the golden shells up on one side of him, and he piles the emeralds up on the other. And as he cracks the nuts, do you know what he sings? He sings the songs of Old Russia."

"Oh, I must see that!" said the Tsar.

But the gnat came and stung the sister in the eye, stung her in the eye so that she screamed with pain, and the boyars all got up and chased the gnat, but they couldn't catch it. Just as they thought they had it, it would fly away and sting someone else; and they let it go.

At last the gnat came back to Prince Guidon's own shore, and the swan met him and said, "Why are you unhappy?"

"Because," he said, "I heard there of something more marvelous than my city."

"What did you hear of?"

"Well, I heard of a squirrel. A little squirrel that sits and cracks nuts. The nuts have shells of gold, but the kernels are emeralds. And he piles the golden shells up on one side of him, and he piles the emeralds up on the other. And as he cracks the nuts, he sings the songs of Russia."

"You're unhappy for that?" she said. "Don't be unhappy. Go on up to your palace."

And he went on up to his palace, and there outside the gate – there outside the gate of his palace was a great crowd of people and they were looking at something and laughing and singing for joy. And there in the midst of them was a little squirrel. And it sat there cracking nuts, and the nuts were of gold and the kernels were emeralds, and as it cracked them it sang the songs of Russia.

Not very long after that some more ships were washed up on the shore. Prince Guidon came down to the shore and brought the sailors up to his palace, and he gave them a great feast such as they'd never seen nor dreamed of before. And he asked them who they were and whence they came.

They said, "We come from the other side of the world. We are the sailors of the Tsar Saltan, and we've been on the other side of the world gathering spices for him."

When they were ready to leave, Prince Guidon said, "Go and tell the Tsar Saltan of what you have seen here in my palace. Tell him to come and visit Prince Guidon."

As they sailed away he watched them go and tears ran down his face. And again the swan came, and beat her wings, and he was covered in a great mist. And when the mist died away he was a bee, and he flew up, and so he followed the ships. And he followed the sailors up to the palace. And when they came in, there was the Tsar as before, sitting with his head in his hands, very unhappy – and his two sisters-in-law, one on each side of him.

He said to the sailors, "Welcome, welcome back, my men! Where have you been?"

And they told him all the marvelous things they'd seen; and then they said, "And we saw a city in the middle of the blue sea-ocean where no city was before, and outside the city wall a little squirrel was cracking nuts. And the nuts were gold and emerald, and as they cracked he sang the songs of Russia."

"I would like to see that, I would like to see that!" said the Tsar.

"Well, Prince Guidon wants you to come and see him," said the sailors.

"A foolish thing, a foolish thing," said the younger sister-in-law. "A silly thing, for sure! A little squirrel that cracks nuts! What has a Tsar to do with that?"

"Well," he said, "I would like to see that."

But the other sister told of a greater marvel. The bee was so angry that the bee stung her. And this time the courtiers wouldn't even get up to chase it because they remembered what had happened with the gnat. The bee stung hard before it flew out.

When the bee got back he turned into Prince Guidon again. The swan said to him, "Why are you so unhappy?"

"I heard of a marvel," he said. "I heard of a marvel and I want it for myself. I'm alone."

"What did you hear of?" she asked him.

"I heard of a maiden — a maiden who is so beautiful that the sun is not radiant beside her. A maiden so beautiful that she walks with the majesty of a swan, and anyone who sees her knows that she is a king's daughter. A maiden so beautiful that if you part her blond braids of hair you can see the moon shining on her forehead. I want her. I want her for my own. But maidens like this could not exist."

"Oh, she exists," said the swan. "She exists. There is such a maiden. But are you sure that you want her? Are you sure you want her? A maiden is not a glove to be worn or tossed away when you're tired of her. A maiden has a heart."

"Oh," he said, "if I had her I would be faithful to her all my life."

"Very well," she said, and she began to flap her wings. And a great mist enveloped her. And at last she stopped flapping her wings and the mist died away, and he saw before him a maiden so beautiful that the sun had no radiance beside her — a maiden who walked with the majesty of a swan, and could only be a king's daughter – a maiden whose loveliness he wanted to gaze on and gaze on for the rest of his life.

And he said to her, "Will you marry me? Will you come to my mother and receive her blessing?"

And she put her hand in his, and they went up together to his mother. And his mother held the holy icon above them and gave them her blessing, and they were married. And they lived together very, very happily.

And he said to her, "My cup of happiness is almost full. If only I could have my father's blessing."

Not very long after that some more ships came that way, and Prince Guidon went down and brought the sailors ashore. And he led them up and he showed them his palace. He showed them the squirrel cracking the nuts, he showed them his beautiful wife, and he feasted them.

And then he said, "Go back – go back to the Tsar Saltan, and tell him that Prince Guidon sends his greetings and when, when is he going to come?"

So they went away – but this time Prince Guidon did not follow. They went home, to the palace of the Tsar, and they came bursting in before him where he sat between his sisters-in-law. And they said to him, "We have seen marvels, we have seen marvels!" And they told him of the city on the island in the sea. They told him of the squirrel. And they told him of Prince Guidon and his bride whose beauty was such that no man who has ever seen it wanted to look at anything else for-ever.

And the Tsar said, "I will go! I will go and see this marvel."

And the two sisters-in-law together said, "Why do you want to go and see an island in the sea? And a palace on an is-land in the sea? That is for sailors – ignorant sailors. As for the squirrel – that is for children, a squirrel cracking nuts! And as for the maiden — why should a maiden wear a moon on her forehead? We don't want to go."

"Don't go then!" said he. "I am a Tsar! Why am I at the bidding of a lot of women? I am going and you can come or not as you please. Follow me if you want to."

They followed him across the blue sea-ocean and came to the shore. Prince Guidon, alone, came down to meet them. He greeted the Tsar Saltan. He greeted the sailors. He led them up, up to his shining palace, past the squirrel. He led them into the throne-room — and there, his wife came towards them in all her beauty, and leading by the hand her mother-in-law.

And the Tsar looked at his queen, and he looked at his daughter-in-law, and he looked at his son — a hero with the mark of the Lord upon him. And he said, "Who has done this thing?"

And Prince Guidon said, "She whom the gnat stung, and she whom the bee stung."

And then the Tsar said, "Let them be put to death, let them be put to death immediately!"

And they fell on their faces and they begged for mercy, and he said, "Let mercy be done to you as you did it!"

But his wife came forward, and she knelt before him, and she said, "My lord, we were sisters together in my father's house. Spare them."

"Very well," he said, "I will spare them if they go away and I see them no more."

So they went away, to be seen no more.

As for the Tsar, he stayed there feasting and rejoicing for many days. And then he went home to his own palace, and he took his wife with him. But Guidon, he stayed in his shining palace with his radiant wife, and he was a wise ruler and a mighty hero, greater than his father.

The Golden Apples of Lough Erne

ONCE LONG AND LONG AGO, when the ancient districts of Innisfail took their names from the king who ruled them, there lived in the West a king called Conn. His land stretched from Rathlin Island in the North down to the mouth of Shannon – all that way. And he was not only powerful but he was wise, and good, and loved by his people. He had a queen, a Breton princess, named Eda. And if Conn lacked anything, any virtue, Eda made it up.

In their day the earth bore rich crops, their trees hung heavy with fruit, their lakes and rivers teemed with fish, and their herds were abundant. This good couple was blessed with one son. And they called him by both their names. He was Conneda. And the people said of him that he inherited all the good qualities of both his parents.

King Conn and Queen Eda lived in glory many years, and then suddenly sorrow struck, for the queen fell ill, and within a week she was dead. And the king, and the prince, and the court, and the people mourned her with great sorrow for a year. But at the end of that time the king's counsellors came to him and they said that it was not fitting that a king should be any longer without a queen. And they advised him to take to himself as a queen the daughter of his Chief Druid. So he married her. She was a beautiful woman. She had great knowledge, she was wise, and at first all went well.

But after a while she had sons of her own, and as they grew up she suddenly began to realize that though they were fine young men, they were not as well loved as Conneda was. And she realized also that when the king died, her sons would not have a chance of succeeding, but Conneda would inherit the kingdom. And the more she thought about it, the more jealous she became. And at first she tried spreading rumours and scandal about the young prince, but the court and the people just mocked her. They thought it was quite ridiculous, for they knew Conneda.

And then she knew that she must do something stronger than this. So she went to her henwife, and she told her her story and asked her for help. Now the henwife, of course, was skilled in magic. And the henwife said to her, "What would be my payment, if I told you what to do?"

And the queen said to her haughtily, "What payment do you require?"

And she said, "I would like my house filled with wool, and my brother's house filled with red wheat."

"It shall be yours."

And the henwife stood there with her arm at the door. And the queen packed in wool till the house was quite full, from the floor to the roof. And then she made a hole in the roof of her brother's house, and the queen came with red wheat and she filled the house full, from the floor to the roof.

"And now," the queen said to her impatiently, "now tell me what to do."

And the henwife said, "Here is what to do. Here is a chessboard and chessmen. Take them, and challenge Conneda to a game of chess. But first you must agree with him on something. You must agree that whoever wins will choose what he wants as a reward. And you will win. And when you have won, send Conneda to find for you, within a year and a day, the three golden apples that grow by Lough Erne. And to bring home to you also the little black magic horse, and to bring home to you also the little magic hound that belong to the King of the Firbolgs who lives in Lough Erne. Within the space of a year and a day he must bring these all to you, and if he does not, he will be either exiled forever, or he will lose his head."

So the queen thanked her, and she went to challenge Conneda to the game. And he agreed, and they played the game and the queen won, as of course the henwife had told her she would.

But then, not content, she decided that she would really make quite sure that she had Conneda in her power forever. So she challenged him to a second game, and they played a second game, and to her intense astonishment, Conneda won. And then she didn't know what to do.

And Conneda said to her, "Well, you state your reward first, because you won the first game, and then I will state mine."

"My demand, that I put on you and impose on you," said the queen, "is that you procure for me within a year and a day three golden apples from the gardens of Lough Erne, and also the little magic hound from the lake of the Firbolgs, and the little black horse. If you fail at it," said the queen, "you lose your head, or you go into exile for as long as you live."

"Very well," replied the prince, "and my demand on you is that you sit on the pinnacle of this tower until I return, taking no nourishment but so much red wheat as you can lift with your bodkin. And if in a year and a day I have not come home, you are at liberty to come down. But not till then."

43

Conneda was very alarmed at the task that had been put upon him, for he had no idea at all how to set about it. But he decided to go and ask advice of the Chief Druid, who had always been a friend of his. So early the very next morning he started upon his way, but as he left he had the satisfaction of seeing the queen mount to the top of the high tower, where she was to sit till he came home again. And he found his way to the Chief Druid's house, and he was received with great kindness and friendship as always, there at Sheve Bann. His feet were bathed with warm water, and he was given the *fáiltige*, the cup of welcome. And then, when he had rested for a little while, they brought him a meal of the freshest fruit and the oldest wine. And then his friend the Chief Druid asked him why he had come. And Conneda told him.

The Chief Druid said to him, "That is a very hard task that has been put on you. And whoever laid it on you intended that you should not return. I, at the moment, am not in a way to help you. But if you will rest for the night here, I will go in the early morning and consult my druidship."

And early, early in the morning, he went to his green place, and there he consulted the magic that was his druidship, his religion.

And he came back to Conneda, and he said, "My dear son, I find that this is indeed an almost impossible task that has been laid upon you, intended for your destruction. The queen who laid it on you had advice from her henwife, and her henwife is a mighty, mighty druidess of great wisdom. And she is own sister to the King of the Firbolgs, who rules the lands underwater, the lands beneath Lough Erne. I have not the power to interfere for you. The only thing I can do is send you to somewhere where help, if there is help, will be found. I want to send you to the Great Wise Bird with the human head, who knows all things past, present and to come. It is hard to find his hiding place or to persuade him to talk. But I can help you in that matter."

And he called a little horse, a little shaggy horse, and said to the prince, "Mount this little horse, and let the reins hang loose upon him. Do not attempt to guide him – let him guide you. He will take you to the place where the bird is to be found. And in case the bird refuses to help you, I will give you this stone. You present it to him, and he will help you. But you must go at once, for the bird is due at the place where we hope to find him in three days. So go now."

Prince Conneda gave his heartfelt thanks to the druid, and he took the precious stone and he mounted the little horse. He let the reins lie loose upon him, and off they set, more hopefully now. Time will not allow the telling of what they did in those three days – it was a long journey, and they went fast. But the little horse could speak. He could speak a human language, and before the three days were up, Prince Conneda had found a friend.

And at last, at the appointed time, they came to the hiding place of the wise bird, and then Conneda came to him and presented him with the stone as he had been told to. And then he posed his questions as to how he should proceed with his quest. The bird listened, and then took the stone up in his mouth and flew off to an inaccessible spot some distance away. Here he perched, and he spoke to the prince in a loud, croaking human voice. "Conneda, son of King Conn, remove the stone just under your right foot. And take the ball of iron that you will find under it, and the cup that is there beside it. And then mount your horse again, and cast the ball before you. And have the horse follow that ball, and listen to him, for he will tell you what to do." Having said this, the bird disappeared from sight.

Conneda took great care to do exactly as the bird had told him. He found the iron ball, and he found the cup, and he mounted the horse as he had been told. He cast the ball before him, and the ball rolled on slowly, and the little horse followed it with Conneda on his back, until they reached the banks of Lough Erne. And here the ball rolled into the water and disappeared from sight.

"Get down now," said the little horse, "and put your hand into my ear. You'll find a little bottle there, full of ointment: a magic ointment called *ícce*. It heals everything. Take it and guard it carefully. And you'll find also a little basket. Take it and keep it too. And mount me quickly now again, because we must go. Your troubles and dangers are about to begin."

Conneda did exactly as he'd been told. He held the ointment in the basket carefully and he remounted at once. The waters of Lough Erne closed over him like mist, like a soft mist over his head. As soon as he entered the lake, the ball reappeared, and it led them until it came to a causeway guarded by three terrible hissing serpents – frightful monsters. The hissing grew louder and louder. It was enough to terrify the stoutest heart.

"Now," said the little horse, "open your basket. And in it you will find pieces of meat. Cast a piece of the meat into the mouth of each serpent, and be careful. Sit tight, sit tight, and don't slip off, for we have to go past the serpents, and it all depends on your throwing the meat safely into the jaws of each one. If you get the pieces of meat straight into the mouths of the beasts we will be all right. Otherwise, we are lost."

So Conneda flung the pieces of meat unerringly into the mouths of the serpents.

"Oh," cried the little horse, "you're a youth – you're a youth who will see victory." And then he sprang aloft, and he cleared the river, and the ford, and the serpents in a single leap. "Are you still mounted?" he cried. "Are you still mounted, my prince?"

And Conneda said, "I have half my energy left. I can still hold on."

"Good, good," said the little horse. "I find you a prince who is bound to succeed. One test is over, but two more remain. Let us follow the ball."

They followed the ball, and after a while they saw before them a great mountain of fire.

"Now you must hold on," said the little horse. "You must hold on tightly and let nothing unseat you, for we are going over that mountain of fire." And then he rose up into the air, and the trembling prince had no breath to answer. "Hold yourself in readiness," said the horse, "hold yourself in readiness for another leap." Up they went, and the prince held on with all his strength, and the horse rose from the earth and flew like an arrow over the fiery mountain.

"Are you still alive, Conneda, son of Conn?" asked the horse.

"Just alive and no more," said Conneda, "for I am scorched all over my body."

"Well, you're such a young man that you're bound to succeed," the horse answered. "Our greatest dangers are over, and I think now we will survive the last. Alight now, Prince Conneda, and rub a little of the ointment onto your wounds. And put the bottle back carefully."

So the prince did as he was told, and as soon as the ointment touched him all the scorching was gone, and he felt fresh and new again. And then they followed the ball, until they came within sight of a great city. There was only one gate, and that was guarded not by armed men but by two great fiery towers, with flames that leapt out and could be seen at a great distance.

"Now, Prince," said the little horse, "alight on this plain and put your hand in my other ear. There you will find a little knife. With this knife you are going to kill me. And when you have done that, you will wrap yourself in my skin, and then you can pass unhurt in and out of the gate. I beseech you, I beseech you, Prince Conneda, as soon as you have gone through the gate and are safe, come right back again. Come right back again, and drive the vultures away from my body. And then, if there is any *ícce* left in the bottle, put it on me. And restore me. And then, give me decent burial, for I have been your friend. This I do for you. All I ask of you in return is the burial."

Said Conneda, "My noble little steed, my friend, my brother. You have been most faithful to me from the very first, and now you would give your life for me. But I am a man, and I am a prince, and I cannot save my own life at such a cost – the life of another."

"Well," said the little horse, "have I ever given you bad advice? From the very beginning, have I ever given you advice that was not good?"

"No," said Conneda, "you have never given me bad advice – but this I cannot do."

"Listen, my friend and brother, listen to me. I have not misled you before and I will not mislead you now. But hear me, son of Conn Mór, hear me, son of the Great Western Monarch. This is the most important of all my counsel to you – the most important of all. Do exactly as I have told you, or a fate worse than death will befall me. And also, if you do not heed my counsel in this, I am done with you. I am done with you forever."

So Conneda took the knife, and turning his head away from the little horse's ear, he tried with a trembling hand to point it at the horse's throat. His eyes were full of tears and he couldn't see what he was doing, but the knife seemed to have a power of its own, as if it knew where to go, and there it went. And he killed the little horse, and it fell at his feet. With showers of tears he took the skin as he had been told, and wrapped himself in it. And then he ran through the fiery gates quite easily, with no trouble at all.

And he found himself in a great and rich city, its proud towers rising to the sky. But he had not a chance to look around because he remembered the last request of the little horse, and he turned and came back with his sword in his hand, and drove away the vultures who were already crowding over the body. And then he knelt down beside the horse, and with tears pouring from his face, he drew out the little bottle of ointment, and he put what was left on the horse's body, and immediately it was restored.

But a strange transformation was taking place. As he rubbed the ointment in, the horse began to come alive, but in a different shape. And suddenly before him stood a handsome young man. A very, very handsome young man. And they fell into each other's arms with tears of joy.

And the one that was the little horse said to him, "Oh, most noble Prince, you are the best sight I have ever seen, and I am the happiest being alive that I met you. Behold me now in my real shape. But I was for a time your little shaggy horse. I am brother to the king of this city, the King of the Firbolgs. I was enchanted by the wicked druid, to whom you went for help. But when you came to him for help he had no choice but to give you advice that would help you. Come with me now, my friend, and meet my brother, and get the apples, and the little horse and the hound that you are to take home, which will be most gladly given to you."

So they went hand in hand into the city, and they were received with joy by the king and his chieftains and people, and

49

Conneda was deluged with gifts and promises of friendship. And he stayed there until his year and a day were nearly over. Then he took the golden apples, and the magic hound, and the little black horse, and he went home with no hindrance all the way to his father's kingdom.

And he came within sight of his father's house, and there was the queen sitting up in the tower and preparing to come down, for it was almost a year and a day and he had not returned. And she looked down, and who should she see coming along the road but Conneda, with horse and hound and the three golden apples? And in her fury and frustration she threw herself from the tower, and she never troubled anyone again. But Conneda came home in triumph, and his father received him in joy. And after his father's death, he ruled the land instead. The golden apples still grow there, and the land is still called Connaught after that great and mighty king.

Bewitchment

The Woman of the Sea

ONE EVENING a young man was walking down towards the sea in the Island of Unst. He'd been working all day in the fields, and he was very hot and tired. And as the moon was full and there was a cool breeze off the sea he thought he could get cool there. As he came down towards the sea he saw the whole strand glowing white in the moonlight. And there! – there were the people of the sea dancing.

He'd never seen them before. They don't appear often. When you see them in the daytime they're always clothed as seals. But now, because it was midsummer and the moon was full, they were dancing for very joy in the sands, and they'd thrown off their sealskins. And the skins were lying in dark heaps here and there on the sand. But they were so lovely, the sea-people. They were almost transparent. They were clear as the moon itself. And they left no shadows.

The young man had a shadow that went before him. He came down as far as he could without their seeing him and watched the dance, fascinated. But his shadow had gone before him and suddenly one of the dancers stepped on the shadow. And then, of course, the dance stopped. And they all ran to find their sealskins. They ran as fast as they could to the sea – and

53

with little whimpering sounds, little hushed sounds, little bits of chatter, they dove into the sea and were gone. All except one, and she ran up and down wringing her hands and crying, looking everywhere. And he realized she had lost her seal's skin.

And then in the darkness of his shadow, he saw it. He picked it up and he threw it behind a rock to hide it, and he waited.

She went down at last to the sea, and she stood there with her feet in the sea, looking out and calling to her people to wait for her. But they'd gone too far, they couldn't hear her. And at last she put her face in her hands and wept most bitterly. He couldn't bear it, he couldn't bear it. He went up to her and he said, "Woman of the sea, what have you lost?"

"Oh sir," she said, "sir, give it to me. Give it to me. And my people and I will give you the treasure of the sea."

But he said to her, "I'd rather have you than all the treasure of the sea. I'd rather have you." And nothing that she could say would make him change his mind. He said to her, "I want to marry you. I'll take you from here to the priest, and then I'll take you home with me and you'll be mistress of everything I have. Everything that is mine. And on the dark, cold winter nights you won't have to be down at the bottom of the sea. You'll have the stout walls of my cottage around you. And you can sit by your own fire, and be mistress of it. And you'll never have to go back into the cold sea again."

And she tried to tell him about the bottom of the sea – how it was warm there as a river in summer. And how the green sea was over them. And all the treasures were with them, and how they danced and were happy. But he didn't hear her. He wouldn't listen. And at last he threw his cloak around her, and he picked her up and he carried her off to the priest's house and they were married.

And then he took her home, to his own little thatched cottage with the earthen floor. And he showed her the peat fire. And she cried out when she saw it. She thought it was some strange dancing jewel. And he said to her, "Isn't it bonny — isn't it bonny? Have you anything under the sea as bonny as that?"

And she looked into the fire, and for the first time she stopped crying. And in a low, low voice she said to him, "No."

She always loved the fire. As long as she was with him it was the thing she went to most. And when her children were born, her three children — for she bore him three children in the twice seven years she was there — as soon as her children were born she took them to show them the fire.

She was a good wife to him. She baked his bread. She spun the wool from his Shetland sheep. She did everything she should do. And he thought she was content. Certainly she loved the fire, and she was happy with her children.

One day — one day when he was out on the headland plowing, he looked down and saw her by the side of the sea. She was talking to a great seal that was there. "Well," he thought, "I won't say anything to her about it. It's no wonder that she's homesick for her own people." So he didn't say anything about it, and he never mentioned the seal's skin to her. It was never named between them at all. He thought she was content. As for the seal's skin, he had hidden it well.

One night — one night when he was out in the fields and the children were playing between the haystacks and she was in the house baking the bread, she suddenly heard the children crying, "Look, look, look!" they said.

And she ran out to them. "What have you found?" she asked.

"It's like a big cat," they said, "only it's softer and bigger." And they held out her seal's skin to her. They had found it under the hay.

She took it in her hands and she stood there looking at it a long, long time. The children had run away again and they were playing in the gloaming among the haystacks. She could hear their voices like little birds. And the hens had gone to their roost. Every little while one would cluck in its sleep. And the swallows were talking to each other in little chattering voices under the eaves. And from the open door of the house came the sweet smell of baking bread.

And she was about to turn and go in, when suddenly, suddenly there came to her a little soft breeze. She had felt it many times before. She had heard it many times before, but she had never thought of it. Now, in it suddenly she heard the great boom of the waves as they crashed far out at sea. And she heard the little cries of the wavelets as they ran out from the shore to meet them. She heard the whole sound of the sea. And she suddenly took the seal's skin and put it on herself and ran with all her might down the path. And the children came running after her and said, "Wait, wait, wait for us!" But she was gone too fast.

And their father came in from the byre and said, "Where's she gone? Where's she gone?" But before they could even answer he was after her as fast as he could go. But by the time he got to the water's edge she was in the water, and a great seal was with her.

And she turned round, and she said to him – in her voice that was like the sound of the wind in a seashell – she said, "Farewell. Farewell, you've been a good man to me, and I wish you only well." Then she turned and was gone. He stood there with his children. He thought she would come back. They waited, and they waited. But they never saw her again.

The Seven Wild Geese

ONE SPRING DAY, a king and queen were walking in their garden. They were walking by a blue pool, and all around it the broom was yellow. And a white swan had come to the blue pool. The queen sighed, and she said, "If only I might have a daughter who showed the colours of this spring day – eyes blue as the blue pool, hair gold as the broom, and skin white as the swan. If I might have her, I wouldn't care if all my seven sons went off with the wild geese."

"Hush!" said her husband. "Oh, hush! You ask for doom and doom may be sent you."

And she shivered, and he took her home.

And that night, the servant said, "A grey man came and circled twice around the young princes and said to them, *If it be as your mother said, let it be as she asked.*"

And before the spring came again, before the white swan came back to the blue pool, before the broom was yellow, the queen gave birth to a child. And it was a little girl. And when the servants came to tell the king the news, he turned to his sons and he said, "Oh, my sons, may you be with me always!" But even as he said it, a great wind came and blew them out of the house, right across and outside the door and up the little

57

hill outside, where they spread their wings as wild geese and flew away into the empty hills.

The king sent all his noblemen and all his servants out to search, but no one brought any word of his sons. And the king and queen were left alone with just one child, a little girl whose name was Sheen. Sheen means "Storm"; and they called her "Storm" after the storm that took her brothers away on the night that she was born.

And after a while, my listeners, the queen died, and then the king forgot all about his child. He left her to the servants to be brought up, and she was all alone.

And one day — one day, she went out to gather berries with her two friends, the woodman's daughter Mor, and Siav, the foster child of the basket maker. And she came to a place where the berries were rich and red and thick, but as she gathered them, her feet sank into the bog. She sank deeper and deeper, and she pulled and pulled, but she couldn't get herself out. And she cried to her friends, "Help me! help me!" But they didn't hear her.

Her cry startled a flock of wild geese who were hidden in the rushes nearby, and they came and looked at her. And she said, "Help me! Save me — please! Get me out of here."

But they said to her, "You're a girl. If you were anyone but a girl we would help you. But we can't help a girl — for it was all because of a girl that we were driven from our home, from our human forms, and from the company of our father."

And then she knew who they must be. For she had heard the story from the servants. And she said to them, "All my life as long as I can remember I have been sorry about this. Sorry because it was my fault, though I meant nothing. Please, please, help me, and I will do anything I can — anything at all — to help you." And she seemed so earnest and so sorry that they had pity on her. They bent down and spread their wings, and they lifted her by the shoulders, and they lifted her arms, and they lifted her feet, and they carried her up out of the bog to the dry land on the side. And when they landed there, she got down on her knees before them and she said, "Tell me, tell me please. Is there a way that I can help you?"

And they said to her, "Yes, there is. There is. But it is very long, and very hard, and very tiring."

"Tell me what it is," she said.

"Well," said the eldest, "you'd have to gather the bog-cotton — the light down that grows on the bogs — and you would have to weave the thread into cloth, and you would have to sew the cloth into shirts, and you would have to make seven of them. And all this without speaking a word, or laughing, or crying, or making any sound at all. And when all was done, we could all be saved. But not till all is done can any of us be saved."

"I'll do it," she said. "I'll do it — indeed I will do it."

But they said to her, "Well, if you're going to do it you'd better not go back home. You'd better not go back to where you're known. There's a bog between you now and your father's house. Stay on this side of the bog. A little way away you'll find a small cottage — the cottage of the spaewoman. Go there to her and stay with her. Speak no word to her. Do whatever small service she requires and stay with her till your work is done."

So she left them, and she went over to the spaewoman's cottage. The spaewoman lived by telling people their destinies and reading them their dreams. That is why she was called the spaewoman. The people gave her things for telling them their dreams and fortunes, and she left her land and stock to whatever chanced. Sheen found her sitting on the ground before a pot in the fire. Three birds were eating out of the pot — a cuckoo, a corncrake and a swallow.

The spaewoman took Sheen to be a poor dumb girl, so she brought her in and gave her food and shelter, and in return Sheen did small tasks for the spaewoman. She ground the grain; she brought in the turf; she did all the small work that had to be done about the place. And from noon until sunset every day she gathered the bog-cotton on the bog, and in the evening she spun it into thread, and half the night she spun and wove and sewed. And one shirt was finished. And a second shirt was finished. And a third was finished – and a fourth – and a fifth.

One day, she went out to gather bog-cotton for the sixth shirt. It was the spring of the year and the snow was melting and the sky was blue above her head, and her heart sang so that she felt like singing aloud. She thought to herself, "This is the sixth, and when that's finished, and the seventh, my brothers will have their own forms back again, and I can laugh, and I can do whatever I want to do." And she pressed her hand over her lips to keep herself from singing and crying with joy. And she bent and filled her basket.

In the afternoon, as she turned to come home, suddenly something fell at her feet. She looked down, and it was a white grouse. And then she saw a little distance away a man dressed like a hunter. And a falcon was flying over his head, and it came down and lit on the shoulder of the hunter. She stooped and picked up the grouse. The hunter came towards her. His skin was brown; his eyes were blue as gentian flowers. He spoke to her, but she didn't answer, and he went on his way with the hawk on his shoulder.

But she took the grouse home, and fed it on grain, and she set it up in a little niche on the wall where it would be safe. All night long she lay half-awake thinking of the man she had seen hunting. And every time she wakened up she thought of him again.

In the morning, early, she got up and fed the grouse. She saw it scratching against the wall to get out. She carried it to the door, and opened the door to let it out into the morning air. And there, just by the door, was lying a sword, a bright shining sword. Blue – it was so clear and clean. And she stooped down, for she knew it was the sword of the hunter. And just at that moment around the house came the first soft wind of dawn.

And then the spaewoman came and she saw the sword. She took it up, and hung it in a tree where it would not rust, and she said, "That must belong to the Hunter King that people have seen around these parts. People have seen him in many places." And she hung it up and left it there.

Sheen often stood at the door after that, and watched across the bog to see if something more was coming to her. But nothing came – there was no sign of him. She gathered more bog-cotton. But one night when she came home, back to the cottage, a neighbour woman was there and she was talking. She was talking to the spaewoman. Sheen crept into the house and went to her own room and stood there listening to what was spoken. The neighbour woman said that they had found the body of the Hunter King. They'd found it lying in a wood. And they'd brought him home to her house to be waked. And her eldest daughter had sat up to wake him for the first night. And in the morning she was found with her arm withered. And the second daughter sat up to wake him the second night, and she was found with her arm twisted too. And so now it was the third and last night, and there was no one to watch over his body.

When the neighbour woman had gone, Sheen stood there. And she thought to herself that nothing would ever be the same in the world again if the Hunter King was gone. And she

thought how sad it would be for your last night on earth —
your last night above the ground — to be all alone with nobody
to watch with you. She went out across to the neighbour
woman's house. The neighbour woman stood there in the
doorstep, and she said to Sheen, "Girl, I have a body that
needs to be waked. Will you come in and wake him for me? I'll
give you a comb for your hair in the morning if you'll do so."

Sheen nodded that she would, and she came into the house.
And there in the wake room was the Hunter King. He was lying
in a bed, and his hound lay at the foot of the bed. The woman
and her daughters were watching around him. Sheen was afraid
to go over and look at him, but she forced herself to do it. He
lay there with his eyes closed, and a dish of salt on his breast.

The neighbour woman and her daughters brought candles,
and they lit them. They put them in the windows. They put
them at the head and foot of the bed. Then they went into the
dormer room and went to sleep. And Sheen was left alone with
the Hunter King.

She sat down by the fire and she began to spin. She spun a
thread, and when she had finished she hung it around her neck.
The basket of bog-cotton was by her feet, and she was going to
spin the next thread, but she thought she'd better get up and
find another candle so that she would have one to light when
the others were burned down. She got up to look for the candles, but as she got up all the candles in the room flickered and
went out. The hound started from the foot of the bed. And the
Hunter King sat up. And then Sheen *was* afraid.

But she forced herself to go over to him, and she took the
salt that was in the dish, and she put it on his lips. And he said
to her, "Girl — fair maiden — can you follow me? Can you follow me wherever I go? Can you put your hands on my shoulders and come with me? We have to go across the Quaking

Bog. We have to go through the Flaming Forest. We have to cross the Icy Sea. Can you come with me? Put your hands on my shoulders if you can."

She put her hands on his shoulders, and a wind came. And it blew them up the chimney and out onto the ground outside. And as soon as they were on the ground outside, the Hunter King moved a few steps away from her, and she followed him wherever he went. Suddenly under her feet the ground was quaking – but he moved ahead of her, leaping from tussock to tussock, and she knew that they were in the Quaking Bog. Somehow she scrambled after him, falling, pulling herself up, falling again and dragging herself up. But she never let him out of her sight. And she followed him. And there ahead of her she saw a fire, and she knew they were approaching the Flaming Forest. They came out on the other side of the bog. And the fire burnt her cheeks. The fire singed her hair. The fire dropped great burning logs in front of her as she walked. And ahead of her he went, but she never, never let him out of her sight. She never stopped. She went on till they came out on the other side. And they looked down, and there far below them was the Icy Sea. He leapt; she leapt after him. The waters closed over her head, but she kept on swimming. Ahead of her she saw his head bobbing and bobbing on the water, and she followed after till they crossed the Icy Sea.

He said to her, "Fair maid, put your hands on my shoulders again." And she put her hands on his shoulders, and the wind bore them up and dropped them down the chimney of the neighbour woman's house. And there inside as they came in, all the candles suddenly flickered and light came on them again. And the hound stood up – stood up to welcome them – and there was the corpse sitting where they had left it – very, very stiff, but its eyes were open. And he said to her, "Maiden, fair maiden, that was my soul that you followed. That was my soul that you followed through the Quaking Bog, through the Flaming Forest, through the Icy Sea. And you have saved me. I tell you, an enchantress — a wicked enchantress — came this way. She saw me; she loved me — and when I would have none of her, she cast a spell upon me. She said I must hover half way between life and death until I could find a maiden who would follow my soul through the Quaking Bog, through the Flaming Forest, through the Icy Sea. And now you have done all these and restored my soul and my life to me."

Sheen put her hands over her face, and she turned and ran out of the house as fast as she could go back to the spae-woman. All that night she sat up and she finished the threads for the sixth shirt. And she wove them, and then next she sewed them. And the sixth shirt was finished.

On the day after that, she took her basket and she went out to gather the bog-cotton for the seventh and last shirt. And as she was coming home with her basket full, she met the Hunter King. He said to her, "Maiden, is there anything that holds you to this place?" She showed him the basket with the bog-cotton in it. "Come with me," he said. "Come with me back to my kingdom and be my queen, and be the love of my heart."

And the next night she went with him on his horse with the basket in her arms back to his kingdom. And now Sheen was the wife of the Hunter King.

She would have been happy — she would have been very, very happy — except for his three sisters who were jealous of her and hated her. They followed her wherever she went. They watched everything she did. They watched her as she spun. They watched her as she wove. They watched her as she was sewing. They whispered to each other about her, and they told every-one that the reason she never spoke was because her tongue was such a base one it would reveal her humble origins. But Sheen went on with what she had to do, and she was happy. She finished the spinning; she finished the weaving, and now all that she had to do was put the last stitches in the seventh shirt. She longed for the moment when that last shirt would be done, and she could be with her brothers again, and they would be there when she told her story to the Hunter King. But before the shirt was finished, Sheen's little son was born.

At the time of his birth, the king had to be away mustering his armies in another part of the country. But he left word that she was to be well guarded and never left alone for a moment. The servants were to watch her and the sisters were to stay with her when the child was born.

The sisters watched; the kerns were on watch; the whispering maids were on watch; everyone was watching. But on the third night – the third night after the child's birth – music played around the house, such music that everyone who heard it fell asleep. Sheen fell asleep, and her child with her. The sisters fell asleep where they watched. The whispering maids stopped gossiping and fell asleep, and the kerns on duty fell asleep. Everyone slept. And while they slept, through an open window came a great grey wolf, and he came into the queen's room, and in his teeth he took the baby and carried him out of the window and was seen no more. After a while, the music stopped. And as the music stopped the king's sisters wakened up and they went to tend the baby. And the baby was gone. But the queen still slept. And then they were afraid, those sisters – they were afraid of what their brother would say when he came home and found that the child was gone and that they had slept instead of watching. They talked about what they could do. They killed a little animal and smeared its blood on the queen's pillow, and left the queen sleeping there.

65

The king came home before the queen awoke. The child was gone — there was blood on the pillow.

She wakened, she turned, she reached out with her arms for her baby, and there was no child there. Then the sisters told their brother how the queen had killed the baby and thrown its body to the wolves. The king begged Sheen to tell him what happened. But she only knew that she must speak no word. He watched her and wondered why she wouldn't speak, why she wept not at all, why she showed no sorrow whatsoever. She spoke no word. She just sat there. On the fourth day after the child was taken, she took up the piece of cloth and began to stitch at the last shirt. Then the king could not bear it, and he begged her to tell him, and he said to her, "Tell me — tell me what happened. Tell me, please, what has happened." But she made no answer. She wouldn't speak at all. And then he couldn't bear it that she would neither speak nor weep, and he took her hand and led her out of the palace. He said to her, "Go home. Go home to the people you came from, for I cannot bear it that you won't tell me what has happened to our child."

And then she knew that she was being sent away from her home to which she had been brought, and she gave a little cry before she could stop herself. And the shirt — the shirt that was in her hands turned to dry leaves and was carried away by the wind.

She ran all the way to the spaewoman's house, sobbing and crying, and sobbing and crying, and she told the spaewoman what had happened and that her work was all to do again.

And the next day, she started. But when the first thread was spun, the memory of her child suddenly came to her, and she cried — she couldn't stop herself.

Then the spaewoman came to her and said, "Commit your child to destiny. I had a dream last night, and in my dream the son you lost is in the world, and if the maiden who will come to love him will give seven drops of her heart's blood, the seven wild geese who are your brothers will be returned to their human forms. As for you, make an image of your little lost son. Commit it to destiny. And when you have done that, go home and tell your husband all that you have suffered."

Sheen took the spaewoman's advice. She found leaves, and she made an image of her little boy. She laid it on the roof, and the wind came and carried it away. She watched until she could see it no longer. And then she said goodbye to the spaewoman and started out to seek her husband.

But she met him on the road coming to look for her. And he stopped and said to her, "Do you remember how I met you on the bog?" And she said to him, "Do you remember how I followed your soul?" And those were the first words she ever spoke to him. Then he told her that his sisters had confessed what they had done, and that he had come to ask her to come home. They went back together to his kingdom and she lived there as his queen.

But now, my listeners, the barnacle geese are flying over the house, and by the time that they have passed I must bring to an end this story. But there is still a lot I don't know. For if I have travelled far to find out what went before, I have travelled wide to find out what comes after. And this is what I have heard.

Sheen's lost son wandered in the world. The people who met him called him by many names, but none was his true name. And the wind carried him to many places in search of his true name. It carried him near, and it carried him far, and one day it returned him to the house of the spaewoman. And on that day the spaewoman sent a message to Sheen that she had news of her son.

It was the spring of the year. And as Sheen went along the

river bank towards the house of the spaewoman, she heard a young woman singing. And then she saw her on the other side of the river. Her hair was black and she was very pale. And this is what she sang:

> *A berry, a berry, a red rowan berry,*
> *A red rowan berry brought me beauty and love.*
>
> *But drops of my heart's blood, drops of my heart's blood,*
> *Seven drops of my heart's blood I have given away.*
>
> *Seven wild geese were men, seven wild geese were men,*
> *Seven drops of my heart's blood are there for your spell.*

The girl passed on singing softly to herself, and Sheen hurried to the cottage. And there at the house of the spaewoman, Sheen found her long-lost son. And so great was their happiness that they could find no words for it. And when they could speak again, he gave his mother a small token. The token was a young woman's handkerchief, and it held seven drops of heart's blood – seven drops of heart's blood to return seven wild geese to their human forms.

And then the spaewoman sent her most secret messenger into the far empty hills. The messenger was the corncrake. And one night – on the night when the moon was full – seven wild geese came from those hills. And they came to the house where their sister waited. And she took bread that the spaewoman had made, and she moistened seven pieces, and into each piece she put a piece of the handkerchief that held a drop of blood, and gave it to them. And then Sheen called to the spaewoman, and she called her by her secret name, "O Grania, let my brothers be changed back into men!" And the spaewoman passed her hand over each one, and one by one they became men again — men who wanted above all else in the world to see their father.

But look — the barnacle geese have passed and it is time to bring this story to an end. Sheen's lost son has been restored to her and the seven wild geese are men. But there is one thing left to tell. It is of the girl who gave seven drops of her heart's blood. And if I travel far to find out what went before this unique tale, I will travel wide to find out what comes after. And if I am there before you, I'll tell you what I have heard.

The Korrigan

IF YOU'RE TRAVELLING through Brittany you'll come on many moss-covered fountains. They're very beautiful. But you'll notice that over every one of them there is either a cross or a little statue of the Virgin and Child to guard the fountain. And that's because in the old days people were very frightened of these fountains. They thought they belonged to korrigans; and they were women-spirits. Sometimes you found a korrigan who was very beautiful – a young woman, white-skinned and golden-haired. Sometimes she was an old hag, all wrinkled. And if you didn't cross her or do anything to irritate her, she could often give you a charm or a medicine you needed. People said that they used to be the priestesses to the druids long ago. Other people among the peasants said that they were princesses – Breton princesses – who when Christianity came to Brittany had turned it down; and they were forever damned. Anyway, be that as it may, the korrigans are around the fountains.

Now one day in those olden times there was a farmer's wife, and she went down to speak to her husband in the fields one afternoon and left her baby in the cradle. He was a lovely baby, just about six months old, with hair like ripe wheat and blue eyes like cornflowers. And his mother kissed him goodbye and she straightened the coverlet over him. But she forgot to make the sign of the cross. And she went down to the fields.

And a korrigan passed by, and she saw the open door. She looked in, and she saw the baby, golden-haired and beautiful, and she wanted him. So she just picked him up and took him. And instead she put her own little, wrinkled, ugly *poulpican* in the cradle. And when the mother came home she wondered what was wrong with the child. He'd always been so sunny and sweet; and now he was so cross, oh, so fretful, so peevish — a horrible child. And she said to her husband, "I think there's something wrong with him."

But her husband said, "Oh, he's just changing. Babies do. He'll soon be a child."

But the days went by. He didn't grow much bigger, but he grew much cleverer. And he watched her all the time. He watched her in a spiteful sort of way. And she wondered what in the world was wrong with the baby. She spoke to her husband again and he said, "Well, he's not a baby anymore. He's a little child."

But nothing could satisfy him. And the years went by, and he could walk and he could talk. He never smiled. He never was nice. He never was loving. He was always curious about everything.

One day — one day, a neighbour turned in. It was a wet, wet night, and he'd come from the fair and he'd bought a little calf and he was riding on his horse. And he wrapped his cloak around himself and it fell over the horse; and it was around the little calf in his arms as well. And he delivered his message and, just as he turned to go, he heard the child say,

> *Egg before white hen I knew,*
> *Acorn before oak.*
> *But never before saw I three heads under one cloak!*

Now that, thought the neighbour, was a strange thing because that child was only about six years old, and he's talking like an old, old man. And he told the farmer's wife, and she was even more frightened. And she told her husband, but he brushed it away.

But a little after that she thought she would test him – and she did. One day, she got an eggshell and into it put some oaten porridge, some wheaten porridge, and she stirred them all around and she put them into the pot to boil, all in one eggshell. And he said to her, "Mama, what are you doing?"

And she said, "I'm making supper for your father's workmen."

"Supper?" he said. "Supper?"

"Yes," she said, "this is the way you make supper for workmen."

And he looked at her and he said,

> *Acorn before oak I knew,*
> *Egg before white hen.*
> *But never saw I in one eggshell supper for twenty men!*

Then the mother was really afraid. That night, after the child had gone to bed, she and her husband sat up for a long, long time together and they talked. She told him all of the things he'd said, and all of the things he had done, and how, when she sent him out to milk the cows, he tormented them; how, when she sent him out to mind the chickens, he hurt the chickens:

how he hurt everything that came his way. And how he watched her, watched her, watched her.

"Husband," she said, "he's going to do us some harm, he's going to do us some harm."

And the husband said, "You're right. I thought he was just a boy, and I was a boy once myself. But I didn't do things like he does. I'm going up to his room. I'll take my knife with me. And we'll see what we'll see."

So he went up to the room where the boy was sleeping, and he saw that the boy, though he looked asleep, was not really asleep at all but was watching him under his eyelids. And the husband looked at him for a minute or two, and he pulled out his knife and ran his thumb along the sharp edge of it. And as soon as the boy saw that he let out a screech — such a terrible screech you could have heard it miles away. And hardly had he screeched once when the door was flung open and a woman appeared. And she had by the hand a little boy about ten years old, with hair the colour of ripe wheat, and eyes as blue as cornflowers, and she said, "Take him! Take him! And give me back my own!"

And out of the bed leapt the *poulpican* and into his mother's arms; she took him away. And the farmer and his wife had their own child again, and they lived happily ever afterwards; and they never forgot to make the sign of the cross over him.

To Lose a World

Green Willow

THIS IS THE STORY of Green Willow. Tomodata was a young samurai in the service of the Lord of Noto. He was a beautiful young man, skilled in all the manly arts. He was rich, generous, had a lovely singing voice, was a good dancer, was beloved by everyone. The Lord of Noto loved him too, more than any of his servants. One day he called him and he said, "Tomodata, I need a message taken. Do you love me?"

"You know, my Lord," said Tomodata, falling on one knee.

"You are faithful to me?"

"You know, my Lord."

"You will take a message without fear?"

"You know, my Lord."

"Very well then," said the Lord of Noto, "take this message and deliver it. Mount your horse and ride, and care not for storm or wind, for hill, for enemy country, for anything that may befall you. Ride and bring me back word. And above all, look no maid between the eyes."

"I will, my Lord," said Tomodata, and he took the message and went out and saddled his horse. And he rode. He rode as his lord told him, up the highest hill, at the highest speed that he could go, fearing not for the enemy country or for any other danger that beset him. And he rode, and he rode. And on the third day the autumn storms broke and the rain came down in torrents. The wind was like a tornado. And Tomodata tightened his cloak about him and urged his good horse on.

And they went, not stopping or caring, through day and through night. The storm grew worse. The wind swept away many familiar landmarks, and sometimes Tomodata didn't know where he was. The rain grew worse. He was hungry, he was weary, and the horse could hardly set one foot before another.

At last they found themselves on a great plain. Noon – noon was as dark as evening. And the night – the night was as black as the dark night of the dead. He was on a great, wide plain where there seemed to be no human habitation. The wind was sweeping in every direction, all at once. He was weary to the point of faintness, he had eaten no food for days. And he cried to heaven, "Why must I die on this plain with my duty undone?"

Just as he spoke, suddenly the wind swept away a cloud that was over the moon. The moon shone out in all its brightness, and he saw that he was on a great desolate plain, but near him was a little hill. At the foot of the hill was a small, mean cottage. But there was light showing around the door and at the window. And in front of it were three willow trees. He made his way to the cottage and he knocked on the door with his horse behind him. The door was opened by an old woman, who cried, "Who can be out on a night like this? What is it, stranger?"

He said, "Oh lady, shelter me. Take me in and shelter me and give shelter to my horse. I am a samurai. I am in the service of the Lord of Noto, and I ride now on his errand. Please, give shelter for the night to me and my horse, and a little food, for we are weary almost to death."

"Come in," she said. "Come in. Our food is coarse, and our house is small. But what we have we will give you. And look, my daughter has already taken care of your horse."

And he turned his head over his shoulder and saw that behind him a young girl had taken his horse and was leading it away to cover. Her garments were blown about and her long loose hair streamed out upon the wind. He wondered where she had come from, but he followed the old woman in, and she supported him because he was so weak he could hardly get into the house.

Inside the house by the small fire there was an old man. And the two old people got up and they gave him hot *sake*, which warmed his heart, and they took the wet clothes off him and wrapped him in dry blankets and sat him down before the fire. And the woman went to prepare him a supper, a good supper.

After a while the young maiden came in from outside. She retired behind a screen to where she and her mother slept, and she took off her wet clothes, combed her hair, washed her face, and came out and knelt down beside him to pour his wine. She was bent over beside him so he couldn't see her face, but the hair was long and beautiful, right down to her knees. He said to her, "What do they call you, maiden?"

"They call me Green Willow," she said.

"A beautiful name, a beautiful name," he told her, "the most beautiful in the world!" And she looked up, and he looked into her eyes. Alas for his quest! He looked at her for some time, and then he made a foolish song and sang it to her:

> *Long-haired maiden, do you know*
> *That with the grey dawn I must go?*

79

> *Do you wish me far away?*
> *Lovely long-haired maiden, say —*
> *Long-haired maiden, if you know*
> *That with the grey dawn I must go,*
> *Why, oh why, do you blush so?*

And she said to him:

> *Dawn comes if I will or no;*
> *Never leave, never go.*
> *My sleeve will hide the blush away.*
> *Stay, my lord, I pray you, stay.*
> *Look, I lift my long sleeve so.*

All that night he tossed in his sleep, thinking of nothing but Green Willow. "Green Willow, Green Willow," he said to himself, forgetting filial piety, forgetting his duty to his lord, forgetting his honour, forgetting everything that he owed. "Green Willow, Green Willow."

He wanted to do his duty. He strove to drive her out of his mind, but he could think of nothing else. Early, early in the morning he awoke. He got up, washed himself and dressed, and went very quietly over to where the old man lay still asleep. He left a purse of gold beside him in thanks for what the man had done for him. And without any further word he crept out.

The rain had ceased, the wind had stopped. The whole earth was washed and new. It was fresh and dewy, and bright and lovely. He mounted his horse and rode, but always as he rode he thought, "Green Willow, Green Willow, Green Willow." Noon came, and he was still saying, "Green Willow, Green Willow." And at night, when he stopped to rest at a deserted shrine, he was still saying, "Green Willow." But when he got inside the place it was so old and so holy that he forgot, and slept soundly all night long.

He got up very early in the morning, and thought he would go down and bathe himself in the little stream that ran nearby, which would be cold, and then he could go on his way and continue his quest. But as he got to the door of the temple, there across the threshold was Green Willow, lying on her face with her long black hair covering her. And she caught him by the sleeve and she said, "My lord, my lord, do not leave me." She burst into tears. There was nothing that he could do.

He picked her up, he wrapped his cloak about her, he set her on his horse, and they rode away. They rode all day, not knowing where they were going, not caring. They rode for another day, and on the third day they came to a city. And here they decided to stay. Tomodata had money with him. He bought a house, a little house that was just newly painted – white – and all things were whiteness. The steps were white; there was a garden around it.

And here they dwelt for a year, and another year, and part of another year in great happiness. And then – then one September night they went out together into the garden to look at the moon, which was shining full and bright in the sky. Suddenly she began to shiver. And he said to her, "Come inside, the night air is chill. Come in and get warm."

"No," she said. "No. Say a prayer for me, Tomodata, for I am dying."

"No, no," he said. "It's only the chill of the night. Come in; you will be well."

But she said, "No, no." And she turned and clung to him and she said, "My lord, my lord, somebody has cut down my willow tree. My lord, I die." And she slipped through his arms and fell to the ground. And he knelt down beside her, and there was nothing there but a little pile of sweet scented silken clothing, and a pair of little straw sandals with scarlet thongs.

Years later, after he had become a holy man and travelled up and down the land from shrine to shrine, he came one night late to a great, empty plain with no human habitation upon it that he could see. And there in front of him was a little cottage – a little cottage all broken down and worn away. The door was off its hinges. The windows were broken, and in front of it were the stumps of three old willow trees. He looked at it and he began to sing,

> *Long-haired maiden, do you know*
> *That with the grey dawn I must go?*
> *Long-haired maiden, will you say,*
> *If you know I must go away,*
> *Why, oh why, do you blush so?*

"Foolish song," he said. "Foolish, foolish song. I should have recited the Holy Sutra for the Dead."

The Golden Fly

ENGUS AND FUAMACH and Midyir and Ethaun lived in the World of the Gods. But Ethaun was restless. "Take me with you Aengus," she said. "Take me with you when you go into other worlds."

"No, I can't do that," he said, "because when I go into other worlds, nobody knows that I'm a god. They think I'm just a travelling musician. I do magic. I'm a juggler. You would be just a poor singing woman. No one would respect you."

"Well," she said, "I'm sick of everything I see. I will ask Midyir to make a world for me."

So she went to look for Midyir, and as she went she passed over the dark shadow that is Earth, and the bright shadow that is Ildathach. But when she came to Midyir he was leaning down, looking at Earth. And when he smiled, he made a brightness on the darkness of Earth. And it made Ethaun angry, that he could spend his time smiling at the Earth. And she said to him, "All the worlds are full of weariness. I wish they would clash together and there would be an end of them."

"You know," said Fuamach, "you have the heart of a fly. You are never content. Be a fly, until you find a world for yourself." And as she said it, suddenly Ethaun was a little golden fly.

She flew to Midyir and she buzzed around him but he just brushed her away, and went on looking down at Earth. So she came back to Aengus. He was playing on a *tiompán*, and she buzzed around him and he said, "Oh, you're a beautiful little fly, you are beautiful. And you make a pretty buzzing. I will give you a gift – you shall have whatever you want. And I'll give you a voice to ask for it."

So he gave her a voice. And she said to him, "Oh Aengus, I am Ethaun. Fuamach has turned me into this little golden fly because she said I had the heart of a fly. Aengus, give me back my own shape again."

But Aengus said, "I can't do that. It's only in Ildathach that I am a shape-changer. I'll tell you what I can do," he said. "If you'll come with me to Ildathach I'll build a palace for you there. I'll build you a beautiful palace. And I'll come and visit you, and sing to you. Will you come?"

"Yes!"

So she went with him to Ildathach. And he built her a palace, a most wonderful and beautiful palace. It had four windows. One window looked to the north, and when you looked out of that northern window you saw great mountains, with peaks white as snow. Then there was a window to the west, and if you looked out of that you saw pine trees, and oak trees, and orchards, and trees with golden apples. But if you looked out of the window to the south, there was a land full of little blue lakes. The window to the east looked out on the sea, but she must not open that.

And at first she was very happy in Ildathach and in the palace, and Aengus came to see her and he sang to her, told her stories, and she enjoyed it. But after a while the old weariness came upon her, and she was restless and tired of everything she saw. And one day she said, "It is always the same. It is always the

84

same." And she went to the window in the east, and she opened the shutters, and the sea came pouring in, and the breeze picked her up and carried her out. And the minute she was outside the palace, she was no longer Ethaun, but a little golden fly.

And the wind bore her up and down and over seas, over Ildathach and to Earth, where the sun beat upon her, and the rains lashed her, and the winds blew her. And then at last one day – at last one day she came to a king's palace with a green lawn, and on the green lawn a king and queen were standing and they were drinking golden wine out of golden goblets. And the king filled a glass with wine and passed it to the queen. And just as she was about to drink, the little golden fly settled on the rim of the goblet. And the queen drank her with the wine.

Some time after that the queen had a child – a most beautiful child. A girl child, strangely beautiful. She called her Ethaun. Everyone in the palace loved her because she was so beautiful, and everyone tried to please her. But nothing pleased her for long. And as she grew older she grew more beautiful, and they tried even harder to please her. But she was even harder to please.

And one day – one day the king's minstrel was singing a song, and Ethaun laughed at the song and she said it was a silly song. It had no music to it, and she knew a better one. And she would sing her own song. And she sang her own song. And as she sang, the queen looked into her eyes and she knew that this was no child of hers. She was one of the immortals, who bring to men and women more joy, or more grief, than is good for them. And when the queen knew it, she turned her face to the wall and she died.

Then the king was angry. He said that Ethaun brought trouble and made trouble wherever she was. And he had a little hut built for her deep in the forest, and he sent her out there.

And none came near her, except the simple folk who brought her food and cared for her wants. And she walked up and down under the forest trees and combed her golden hair.

And one day as she was sitting outside her little house, combing her golden hair, the High King of all Ireland, whose name was Eochy, came riding by. And he looked at her and he said, "No woman is beautiful after this one. She has every woman's beauty in her face." He reined in his horse and he said, "Maiden, what is your name, and who is your father?"

"My name is Ethaun," she told him, "and a king is my father."

"And why should you waste your beauty here?" he said. "Why don't you come with me? I am the High King of all Ireland, and I will take you home with me and marry you, and you shall be my queen."

And she looked at him. She looked at him for a long moment and then she said, "I've been waiting here for you for a long, long time."

So he took her home, and he married her, and all the land rejoiced because the queen was so beautiful. And the king rejoiced too. And he built her a palace, a palace of red yew, with jewels set in the walls and in the doors. And she looked at it. But always when she looked, it seemed to her that somehow in her heart she knew of a palace which made this one look shabby. And no one could please her.

To the king's palace came all the great poets and all the great champions, and all the great magicians, and all the great musicians. And the king gave them gold, and at Samhain time, all the harpers of the Five Provinces of Ireland came to Eochy's palace. But no matter how hard they tried, Ethaun was not pleased with what they did. And though the king paid them well and gave them gold they went away dissatisfied.

One day – one day, Ethaun was outside her own quarters, and inside a fool, who was kept in the palace because his wits had gone from him – and people say, you know, that fools have the dark wisdom of the gods – he was inside, strewing sweet-smelling blossoms and rushes on the floor where the queen sat. And as he worked he was singing to himself. He sang:

> *I had a black hound and a white.*
> *The day is long and long the night.*
>
> *A wave came up out of the sea,*
> *But still my hounds were following me.*
>
> *The white hound had a crown of gold,*
> *But none had seen it, young or old.*
>
> *The black hound, he had feet like fire –*
> *'Tis he that was my heart's desire.*
>
> *The sun and moon went from the sky*
> *As I and my two hounds went by.*

Ethaun went into the house. As she went along, her feet crushed the little blossoms that the fool had spread. And her skirt swept them, and she didn't even notice. And she went up to the fool and she said, "It is well for you that is a heart so lightsome that you can sing like that. I would my heart were as light as yours."

"How could your heart be light, O Queen," he said, "when you won't let anything live? You won't give a bud the chance to blossom. You won't give a bird the chance to find its prey. You won't give a dog a chance to chase what it is after. No, Queen –

if you were one of the Deathless Ones you would burn down the world just to warm your hands."

And when she heard that, a dark flood of shame came over Ethaun's face, and she bent her head. And she picked up a little bud, and she said, "Every bud that I pick, dies. I will pick no more buds, Fool."

And just at that moment there was a great noise outside, and she called her women to see what it was. And they said, "Oh, it's just a poor strolling player, a juggler, a magician. He's no good, he can't do any tricks. But they're driving him away. He doesn't want to go."

"Let him stay," said Ethaun. "I will come and see his tricks."

"But what good will that do?" said the maids. "Last night – last night Incar, the king's juggler, did his best for you, and you said he was no good. How would this man please you, who is so clumsy?"

"If he tries, he will please me," said Ethaun. And she went out, and there was a poor juggler, and he did his tricks, clumsily. But she smiled at him and was pleased, and he did better tricks.

And in the end she gave him a ring and the little bud that she had picked. He took her ring and he tucked it away in his clothing. And then – then he took the little bud and he breathed on it, and it became a white rose. And one by one he pulled the petals of the white rose and he threw them into the air. And as he threw them into the air, they became white birds and they flew away, and away, and away up into the sky. And all the people stared, and Ethaun stared after them, open-mouthed. And they didn't know the earth beneath their feet or the sky above their heads for joy. Wheeling and wheeling the birds went until they had disappeared. And the people looked for the juggler, but he was gone.

And then Ethaun called, "Aengus, Aengus, Aengus Óg!" But he was gone. And that night – that night Incar, the king's juggler, did wonderful tricks, and Ethaun praised him so that he did better and better ones, till the people could hardly believe it.

And in the middle of all the rejoicing, when it was at its height, there strode a stranger into the hall – a dark stranger, clad in the clothes of a strange land. And the king, who loved visitors and strangers and all sorts of people, said to him, "Who are you, and what can you tell us that we don't know?"

And he said, "I am a stranger from another land, and I can tell you where the sun goes when you don't see it anymore. Oh, and I can play chess."

Now the king loved chess. And he was considered a very good chess player. So he said, "Let the chessboard be brought."

But the servants said to him, "O King, there is only the one chessboard. It is the one that you made for the queen, but she said it was ugly, so it has been put away."

"I have a chessboard," said the visitor.

"I will fetch mine," said the king, and he went to get it. And while he was gone, the stranger brought out his chessboard. It was made of gold and ivory, and the ivory was whiter than clouds, and the gold was redder than the sunset.

And he brought out the men and began to set them up. And he said to the queen, "I will make a chessboard for you."

But she said, "No, I only want the chessboard that Eochy made for me."

And then he looked at her and he said, "I would make a world for you."

And then suddenly she knew him, and suddenly she remembered who she was. And how she had been a little golden fly, beaten up and down by the wind. And she said to him, "Oh, Midyir – oh, Midyir, in all the worlds I would be a stranger, for I have never made a world for myself."

And just at that moment Eochy came back with the chess-board. "What will we play for?" he said.

"We play three games," said Midyir, "the first two on your board and the last on mine, and the winner chooses."

"Agreed," said Eochy. So they played the first game, and Eochy won.

"And what do you want?"

Eochy said, "I want fifty horses out of Faërie."

"They're at your gate now," said the stranger. "Shall we play again?" They played again and Eochy won again. "What do you want this time?" asked the stranger.

"I want the mountains levelled. I want a road built over them. I want the stones out of the fields, and I want rushes growing in the desert place."

"Tomorrow morning, go to the little hill behind the palace and look. And you will see that your will has been done. Shall we play again?"

So they played again, this time on the stranger's board. And this time the stranger won.

"What do you want?" said Eochy.

"I want Ethaun," said Midyir.

"No, no, I won't give you Ethaun," said Eochy. "Anything but Ethaun."

"But the horses of Faërie are at your door already. And the other task is underway. You gave me your word."

"I won't give you Ethaun," said Eochy.

And Midyir turned to Ethaun, but she said to him, "Midyir, Eochy has loved me, and his people have loved me. They have brought me gifts and they have made a world for me. But now I have to make a world for myself. Come back in a year, and I will go with you." And as suddenly as he came, Midyir left.

The year that followed was like no year that ever was in Ireland. The three crowns were on the land – the crown of plenty, the crown of victory, and the crown of song. Ethaun gave gifts to the people, and as for Eochy, she gave to him such joy in one year as few men know in a lifetime.

And at the end of the year he made a great feast – it was Samhain. And all the harpers and all the champions and all the magicians and all the poets were there. And a thousand, thousand candles burned. And into the middle of the feast strode Midyir the Red-Maned. He had a cruit in his hand – the small harp that musicians carry. And he looked around till his eyes found the queen. She was sitting on a silver throne beside Eochy. But as he stood there, all the kings fell to their faces before him. And the great chiefs and the ollavs. Because Midyir had come.

He played on his cruit, and he sang:

> *Come away, come away, Ethaun.*
> *Leave the weary portals of life,*
> *Leave the dune, leave the bawn.*
> *Come! Come! Come! Ethaun.*
> *Lo, the white-maned untameable horses*
>   *outracing the wind*
> *Scatter the embers of day from their hooves,*
>   *and the riders who bind*
> *The sun to their chariot wheels are calling*
>   *your name.*
> *They are calling your name through the night,*
>   *and the night is aflame.*
> *Ethaun! Ethaun! Ethaun!*

Why did you turn from me, from me,
your only lover?
What lure have you found in the eyes of a mortal
whom clay must cover?
Come back, come back, Ethaun.
Lo, the high-built heavenly places mourn for you,
and the lights are quenched.
And for you immortal faces grow wan
as faces that die.
O Flame-Fair Swan of Delight,
Leave behind the portals
of sleep-heavy night.
Lo, the hosts are waiting,
Their horses scatter the embers of day.
Light of a world that is deathless,
Come away, come away.

Ethaun turned to him, but first she went to Eochy and kissed him. "Eochy," she said, "I've put into one year the joy of a lifetime. And tonight — tonight you have heard the music of Faërie, and echoes of it will be in the harp strings of Ireland forever. And as for you, Eochy, you will be remembered as long as grass grows and rivers run. Because Ethaun, whom Midyir loved, loved you."

And she turned toward Midyir, and she put her hands in his, and they rose together as flame rises when it is morning. And in the World of the Gods, Aengus and Fuamach awaited them. And they were together there, the four of them, as they have been from the very beginning.

The Peach-Blossom Forest

IN CHINA, if you see a very beautiful peach tree, you say to the man who owns it, "No doubt you are of the house of Wu Ling?" And there's a story to that. And this is the way the story begins.

One morning very early, before the sun was up, a young man called Ying went down to his boat, leaving the miserable little hut in which he lived right on the edge of the town. None of the other fishermen was up. No doubt they could sleep in because they didn't have elderly parents to support, as he had. But down he went to the water's edge, and on his shoulder was a bird, a great black bird with a bronze ring about its neck. This was his own cormorant, that he had trained carefully and well, all by himself. The cormorant could not swallow the fish he caught because of the ring. But when he had finished his day's work, Ying would give him his own fish, cut up small.

They set off now, down the river and away across the plain. Far, far away the sun began to rise, sending shimmering light over all the river. They saw no one. They were still too early to see anyone else. They passed the rice fields, they passed a bamboo grove, they passed an old, deserted temple. And then they came to a wide stretch of the river. And now they began to fish.

He let the cormorant loose, and it went with its bright eyes darting here and there, not missing a ripple, not missing a shadow in the water. It came back with a fish, and then another. But very, very few. After this hour's fishing they usually had the basket half full, and now there was only a handful of fish lying at the bottom.

And Ying sighed to himself because he knew that his old mother dearly loved a slice of pork to eat on top of her rice, and he would have to catch a lot more fish if she was to have that today. He went a little farther down the river and he saw, off in the distance, peach trees, on the edge of the river. And he let the cormorant loose again and he flew away. This time he came back with a fine, large fish. Ying laid that on top of the rest, and then suddenly something moved him to bring the boat ashore. He tied it up there and tethered the cormorant. He just didn't want to fish anymore.

He got out and started to walk among the peach trees. He didn't know why he walked along that road with the peach trees above him white as down, tinted with red, and the blossoms dropping one by one on his sleeves. And he went on and on. He'd known nothing like this in all his poor, toilsome life. He walked and he walked, not knowing why or where he was going. And then suddenly the forest ended, and there before him was a face of rock. He stopped, he could go no farther. But then he noticed a little crevice in the wall. He went up to it and looked in.

There was a path that led in, and from far away he could hear a sound like girls' voices, but it was dark in there, and narrow. But he went in, feeling his way with his hands along the two sides. Nothing but darkness ahead of him. But he still could hear the chatter of the voices. So he followed the path, and after a while a faint light appeared off in the distance. And then after a while the path widened, so he could only touch the rock with one hand. And he came to where there was an opening, and he stepped out.

There in front of him was a green land. And almost at his feet were two young maidens having a picnic. They were dressed in bright silk dresses with designs of birds and flowers, clouds and waves embroidered on them in gold thread. And they had a little brazier and it made tea which they were drinking out of fine china cups. He had never seen anything like them. Their hair was piled high on their heads, and it was fastened with combs and jewellery. Occasionally when he had delivered fish to the governor's house he had seen pictures like this – but this was all of long, long ago. Five hundred years ago. There was nothing like it today.

The girls were startled. They looked up and they said, "Who are you?" And he couldn't answer; he just stood there. And the one who seemed to be the elder said to him, "I'm Golden Bells, and this is my sister, Summer Dress. What is your name?" And he couldn't answer.

And the younger one said, "Oh, you poor man, you must be ill! Something must be wrong with you. Look, look, Golden Bells, his clothes are all in rags. And he's so dirty he…" Summer Dress realized that she had offended him. He stood with his head hanging, not knowing what to say. And she quickly motioned him to sit down on the grass beside her, and she handed him his tea. And she said, "We are having a picnic here. What is your name and where do you come from?"

"I come from the city," he said. "My name is Ying. I'm a poor fisherman."

"What city?" they said.

"The city," he said.

"We don't know where you mean," they told him. "We live

here. This is our father's country. We'll take you to see our father. You must come and see our father."

"Is he a magistrate?"

"A magistrate!" they said, "what's a magistrate? What strange speech this person has! He uses so many strange words." Well, Ying was glad he was not a magistrate – he had had unhappy meetings with these men, so he was not anxious to meet another. But they said to him, "Come with us, we will take you home and you will meet our father. He is the Lord of Wu Ling." So they took him home.

All the way home people came to the doors of houses all smiling, all happy – all looking so joyful, so innocent. He had seen nothing like them where he came from. They all waved, they all spoke. They led him finally to a compound, and a great house with an outer courtyard. And the people came and opened the gates for them, and led them in. In the courtyard they told him to sit down and rest himself – they would go and speak to their father. And servants came, smiling servants, and waited on him and brought him food – food such as he had never even smelt in the magistrate's or the governor's houses. This was better than anything he ever had. The delicate rice, the tender chicken, the little bamboo shoots, the tea.

At last the two girls came back, and they took him to their father. They knocked on the door and a dry, old voice inside said, "Come in." They let him in and they closed the door behind him, and they went away. And he was alone in the room with an old, old man. "Come in, stranger," said the old man. "You've come from the toilsome world, have you?"

"I'm a poor fisherman. I come from the city."

"Well, you've found your way here. I'm sorry for you. I'm very sorry for you, but you must go away again. You cannot stay here. You must leave us, and go back to the toilsome life again. We have lived here for five hundred years. At that time, long ago, it was a very sad time in China. They were building the Great Wall. Husbands, brothers, nephews, and sons were all taken away to build the wall. But a few of us managed to escape, and we've been here with our people all these years. And our life is serene and happy and peaceful. And nobody knows how to find us.

"You must go back the way you came. And you must give me your word that you will never tell anyone where you have been." Ying was afraid, so he gave his word. He knew in his heart even as he gave it that he would not keep his promise.

The next day – the next day, a great ship came sailing down the river. And on it the magistrate, and the governor, and all the great officials of the city. And Ying. They passed the rice fields, they passed the bamboo groves, they passed the ruined temple, and they came to where the river widens. And they all cried, "All right, show us, show us. Where is the peach-blossom forest? Where is it, where is it?"

"Where is it?" said the magistrate.

"Where is it?" said the governor.

Ying said nothing. He just looked, and looked, and looked. Ahead of him was the wide river and the mud flats. But no peach trees. No peach trees at all. They were all gone.

> Some day, fishing for the thousandth time,
>   you will find it –
> The peach-blossom forest, the cleft in the rock,
>   the house of Wu Ling.
> Oh do not betray it. Hold on to it.
> Keep it in your heart, and it will blossom.

Wives and Husbands

The Good Wife

T HERE WAS, there was, and yet there was not. There was a lazy man, and he married a good wife. The whole spring long she pleaded with him to get his crops sown. She worked, and she pleaded, and she begged, and at last, by the time summer came all his crops were in. And he lay down and rested for the whole summer.

She wakened him in the fall and got him out, and do you know what he did? He cursed the crops, because they had grown so tall. She said to him, "My dear, my darling, take your scythe and go out and cut them." No, he couldn't today, not to-day. He didn't feel like it today.

So the next day she came to him again and she said, "My dear, my darling, cut your crops, do cut your crops." No, he thought that was a cloud up there, he didn't think it would be a good day.

She came to him the third day. "My dear, my darling," she said, "won't you cut your crops today?" No, he had to go and see a man in the next village about something.

The next day and the next she tried, and she had no luck at all. She went to him at last and she brought his scythe, and she put it in his hand and she said, "Come, my dear, let's go down to the fields, and you can cut just a little corner, just a little corner. And I'll go and make you eggs and green beans for your breakfast, and I'll bring them down to you here."

So she left him there with the scythe in his hand and she went home to get the beans and the eggs ready. She looked out of the kitchen window and he was fast asleep in a corner of the field. So she sighed. She covered the fire; she closed the door.

She went over to her father's house. No one was at home. Father and her brothers and all the family were out, of course, in the fields. She went upstairs to her brother's room and she got his black suit that he wore on Sundays to church, and his black shoes. She found some black paper; she made herself a mask. She went out into the stable and got her father's big black horse, and she mounted it. And then she pulled down a whip, a shiny whip from the wall, and off she set.

She came galloping along the country roads, lashing the whip from side to side, and crying, "I am the devil, plague of the lazy! I am the devil, plague of the lazy! I am the devil – take that! and that! and that!"

When she got to the husband, he came awake and he stared up at her and she said, "I am the devil, plague of the lazy. I'm off now to the next village to see about a man who has not cut his crops yet. And I'll be back by evening, and it will be the worse for you if yours aren't cut!" And with a last crack of her whip she went home again.

She put the horse back in the stable, the whip up on the wall. She destroyed the paper mask; she put the suit right back where it belonged. She started the fire again in her own house; she made the beans and the eggs and carried them down to him. He was working – oh, he was working! "Here's your breakfast, my dear, here's your breakfast."

"Oh no," he said. "No, I can't stop now. I can't stop now.

Put it in my mouth! Put it in my mouth! Put it in my mouth!"
So she put his breakfast into his mouth. She cooked his dinner
and put that into his mouth too. Early in the evening he came
home. Everything was cut. He threw himself down on the
couch, and he said, "I'm going to die."

"Oh, of course you're tired," she said. "Of course you're
tired. You'll feel much better after a night's sleep. Just lie and
rest, and I'll bring you some supper."

"No, no," he said. "No, I'm going to die. I can't go on living
like that!"

He couldn't be moved. He sent her out to order his coffin.
They got the coffin, and it was carried down and put in a
church. They ordered the priest. They got the mourners. He
climbed into the coffin and he lay there. She lit candles at his
head, she lit candles at his feet. The mourners stayed the whole
evening long. He was to be buried in the morning.

She waited till midnight. The candles had flickered out. The
mourners had all gone home. The church was dark. She went
and stood just in the doorway and she cried, "I am the angel in
charge of work for the dead! I am the angel in charge of work
for the dead! All new corpses, get up now, and carry ten bricks
to heaven. All old corpses, get up and carry a hundred bricks to
heaven."

She had just time to get home, when there he was. He leapt
out of the coffin and came running home after her as fast as he
could come. "Aren't you going to die?" she said. "Aren't you
going to die?"

"Die?" he said. "Die? Oh no! Not me. I'd rather stay alive
and work for myself, than die and carry bricks to heaven for
somebody else."

The Clever Wife

IN THE OLDEN DAYS there was a great ruler whose name was Sarybay. He ruled his people wisely and well for many years. Then he knew he was going to die. And as he felt death coming on, he called his people to him and said, "My people, I've been your ruler for many, many years. And now my death is coming. And as I have no heir, will you choose yourselves a new khan to come after me?"

And they said, "Oh no, no, Sarybay – no, don't leave us, don't leave us."

But Sarybay said, "Listen, I have drunk what was given me to drink, I've eaten what was given me to eat, I have done the work that was given me to do. Now it is time for me to die. So, choose yourselves an heir."

"Oh Sarybay, if you must leave us, choose us an heir."

"No," he said. "No. The dead are soon forgotten, and the words of the dead are soon forgotten, sooner even. No, choose your own heir."

But they pleaded and they begged, and at last he said, "Very well, if you want it so, I will do it for you. I have a white falcon. When I die she will mourn me. She will mourn me for three nights and three days. She will stay up on her stand and she will not move a foot for three days and three nights. She won't touch food and she won't touch drink. Leave her alone. Don't try to influence her. But at the end of the three nights and the three days, give her food, give her water, and watch her. And you will see what she will do. She will spread her wings and she will fly up, up, up into the air in great, ever-widening circles. Then she will come down again, the circles growing smaller and smaller, and she will hover over the head of one person. That will be your new khan."

So they thanked him and he went home. And within a week he was dead. The people mourned their dead khan. But so did the falcon. She went and stood upon her perch for three days and three nights, never moving a foot. She wouldn't eat. She wouldn't drink. Not a motion did she make. And at the end of that time they brought her food, they brought her water, and they watched her. She moved first one foot, and then the other, and then she spread her wings, and she began to fly – up, up, up into the air in great, ever-widening circles. When she had reached a high point in the sky, she came down again, and the circles grew smaller and smaller. She hovered over the head of a young shepherd, whose name was Bolotbek. Then all the people cried, "Bolotbek is our new khan! Bolotbek is our new khan!"

The old people said, "Look at him, he's only a youth! How would he have the wisdom to be our khan? He's not much more than a boy."

And the rich men said, "Look at him, he's only a humble shepherd. How could he be our khan?"

But the people said, "We asked Sarybay to choose for us. And Sarybay has chosen. Bolotbek is our new khan."

So Bolotbek became the new khan. And he ruled his people wisely too, and well. He was just, he was kind, he was generous.

To those who had nothing, he gave of his own flocks and his own lands. And he settled all matters with great justice.

But as the years went by, the people began to be worried. For he had no wife, therefore no heir. At last they went to him, and they said, "Bolotbek, will you not choose yourself a wife so that we may have an heir, so that when you come to die we will not be left again without a ruler? Why do you not marry? Are there no maidens fair enough among the rich young women of the village?"

"I want a wife," he said, "who is as clever as I am. I want a wife whom I can talk to. I want a wife with whom I can discuss things. Bring me the unmarried maidens of the village up to the palace every day for three days and I will ask them three riddles. And the first one who can answer the three riddles will be my wife."

So they got together all the beautiful rich girls of the village, and they brought them up to the palace, and Bolotbek asked them the three riddles. The first riddle was: "How far is it from east to west?" The second riddle: "How far is it from earth to heaven?" And the third riddle: "How far is it from truth to falsehood?"

All day they tore their hair and they beat their breasts, but no one could answer the riddles, and they went home. The next day early they came up again and he asked them the same riddles. Once again they worried and worried all day long, but nobody could answer the riddles. On the third and last day they came again. They started up early in the morning, and they came to a river where a young peasant girl was rinsing wool. Her name was Danyshman. She looked up and she said, "Ladies, tell me, where do you go so joyously and expectantly every morning, and whence do you come home so sadly every evening?"

They said to her, "Mind your own business, which is rinsing wool."

But one of them, who was kinder than the rest, stayed behind and told her. So Danyshman followed them up to the palace. All day long she watched them as they struggled and struggled to answer the riddles. But none of them could. As they went silently away she said, "My lord, my lord Bolotbek, could I try?"

"Of course you could try," he said. "Anyone can try. How far is it from east to west?"

"I think that would be a day's journey," she told him. "You see, I watch the sun every day, and he starts his journey in the east and finishes at evening in the west."

"You're right," he said, "you're right. And the second riddle: how far is it from earth to heaven?"

"Oh," she told him, "I think about the width of an eye. Because you see the eye looks down and sees earth, and the eye looks up and sees heaven."

"You're right," he said, "you're right. Now, the last riddle. How far is it from truth to falsehood?"

"I think," she said, "that would be about the width of five fingers — about the distance from the eye to the ear. Because you see, the ear hears falsehood, but the eye sees truth."

"You're right," he said, "you're right! And now will you marry me?"

She agreed that she would marry him. But he said to her, "There is something to be written into the marriage contract. Do you agree to this? If you marry me, your wisdom is only for me. It is not to be shared with anyone else. That is the condition of your marrying me. Do you agree?"

"Yes," she said. "I agree."

So it was signed into the marriage contract. And they lived

together, very happily, for many years. And she bore him fine sons, so there was an heir.

But then one day – then one day, a young man committed a crime for which the punishment is death. He had to appear the next day to plead before Bolotbek, and he couldn't think of what to say. So he went to the wise queen and begged her help. And she advised him how to plead.

When he came before Bolotbek the next day he pleaded so well that Bolotbek let him go, but he said to him, "Did you think of that by yourself?"

The young man said, "No, the queen helped me."

Then Bolotbek came storming into his wife's chambers and he said to her: "You've betrayed me. You have betrayed your marriage vow. You swore to me that your wisdom was for me, for me alone, and now you have shared it with another." He said, "I want you out of my palace, out of my city, out of my country, before midnight tonight."

"Yes, my lord," she said. "That is just."

"Yes," he said, "I am a just man. I am a just man. And I have loved you, so I will allow you to take with you anything you like when you leave. Whatever you want most you may take with you."

"Yes, my lord," she said. "Thank you. My lord, would you grant me one more favour? Would you let me tonight, for one last time, cook your supper for you, and would you eat it with me?"

He agreed that he would. So all that day she spent getting his supper ready. She cooked all his favourite dishes just as he liked them best, and she brought up all the best wines from the cellar and poured them for him. And he came to supper and he ate and he drank, and he ate and he drank, and he ate and he drank. And in the end he put his head down on the table and fell fast asleep.

As soon as he was asleep she got an old blanket. She wrapped him up in the blanket. She lifted him onto an old farm cart, and she drove it out of the palace yard, out of the city, and right out of the country.

When he wakened it was the middle of the night and he was cold and the stars were over his head. He said, "Where am I? Who has brought me here? What are you doing with me?"

"My lord," she said, "you told me that when I left your palace I could take with me whatever thing I loved most. My lord, I only love one thing, and that is you."

Then he was sorry. He begged her pardon. He begged her to come back with him. He took the reins from her, and he drove the horse and cart back into his own country, into his own city, into their own palace, where they lived happily all the days of their lives.

The Lazy Barber's Wife

ONCE UPON A TIME there was a barber who was so lazy he couldn't even ply his own trade. When his customers came to him for a shave, he cut their throats. When they wanted a haircut, he cut off their ears. Pretty soon, he had no customers left. He grew poorer every day, until at last there was nothing in the house but his wife and his razor, and both were as sharp as sharp can be.

When his wife found out that her husband had no work, she said to him, "Well, you needn't think that *I'm* going to starve. If you can't work, you'll have to beg."

"Beg?" he said. "Beg? Beg?"

"Yes," she said. "Go to the king and ask him for something."

So she sent him off to the king, and away he went. And he begged to the king to give him something.

"Something?" asked the king. "What thing?"

"Oh, I don't know," said the barber. "Just something to have, because I haven't anything."

"Would a piece of land do?" said the king.

"Why, yes!" said the barber. "That would do nicely. It couldn't get lost or run away."

Now the king had an old piece of waste land outside the city that he didn't know what to do with. So he had a deed written out for the barber, and he gave him that. And the barber came home to his clever wife, and she said to him, "Well, what did you get? Give it to me quick so I can go and buy bread with it."

And you can imagine how she scolded him when she found out he had only got a piece of waste land. "You idiot! You fathead! You dolt!" she said. "A piece of waste land?"

"Land is land," said the barber. "It can't run away. We'll always have something."

"Was there ever such a dunderhead?" said his wife. "What good is land unless we can till it? And where are we going to get bullocks, anyway, to till the land for us?"

But, being as I have told you before a very clever woman, she sat down and thought about it for a while.

And then she came to him and she said, "Now, listen to me. Do what I tell you exactly. We're going out to that land, and whatever you see me do you follow me and do the same thing. But don't on any account say anything."

"All right," said the barber.

So they went out to the land, and the wife began to walk up and down the land, peering into it, and peering into it, and peering into it. And then if anyone passed, she would pretend she wasn't doing anything, and look up at the sky. And the barber followed her, doing exactly the same thing.

Now there was a band of robbers nearby. They were in the thicket, and they watched her, and they watched her, and they watched her. And they wondered very much what she was doing. So as the day wore on, they set out to try and discover what she was doing.

"Well, the fact is…" said the barber's wife, after beating about the bush for a while, "– you won't tell anyone, will you? You'll be sure not to tell anyone?"

"Oh, I won't tell anyone," said the robber who had been sent to find out what the couple was doing.

"Well, as a matter of fact, this land belonged to my grandfather, and he was a very wealthy man. And before he died, he buried a great pot of gold somewhere in this land. And then he died before he left any word as to where the gold was. The land's hard and rocky, you see, and I don't want to dig it all up to find the gold. I'm trying to see if we can find, just by looking, the exact place where he put it. Now, you won't tell?"

"Oh no, I won't tell."

"Well," said the barber's clever wife, "we'll be back in the morning to look again."

And all that night those robbers worked. They dug, and they dug, and they dug. They dug up that land from corner to corner and end to end – and not one tiny bit of gold did they find. And they went off very angry and disgusted.

And the next day, the barber and his clever wife came and they planted the land with seed. And all summer they watered it and took care of it. And they had such a fine crop when autumn came that they were able to pay off all their debts, buy food for the winter, and with what was left they bought a big pot of gold, just exactly like the one the wife had described to the robbers.

So they were feeling very pleased, but the robbers were very angry. They were very angry indeed. And they went to the barber's house, and they said, "Give us our share, for we tilled the ground, as you well know."

"I told you there was gold in the ground," laughed the barber's wife. "You didn't find it, I did. I'm the one who found the gold, and there's a crock full of it in the house. Only you rascals will never get a farthing, not a farthing."

"Very well," said the thieves. "Look out for yourselves tonight. If you won't give us our share, we'll take it."

So that night, one of the thieves hid himself in the house, intending to open the door to his comrades when the housefolk were asleep. But the barber's wife saw him out of the corner of her eye. She was determined to lead him a dance. So when her husband, who was in a dreadful state of alarm – he was frightened out of his wits – said to her, "Where did you put the gold? Where did you put the gold?" she replied:

"I put it where no one will find it. You know the big crock full of pickles? Well, I put the gold in that, and I hid it behind the door, and nobody will ever find it."

Now, the robber was hiding, and he heard this, and he waited till he was sure they were asleep. And then he went out and got the crock, and he ran out into the dark with it and the other robbers ran with him out into the forest. And they sat down – it was very dark, and there was no moon that night – and they put their hands into the crock, and what they could find was soft.

"It's the pickles," they said.

"We'd better eat the pickles, and then we'll find the gold at the bottom."

So the robber captain passed around all the things that were at the top of the crock.

Do you know what the barber's clever wife had done? She'd put all the sweepings of the house into that crock. There were dead mice; there were dead rats; there were frogs; there were old vegetables; there were peelings of this and that. And the robbers crammed their mouths full. And then they realized what they had got, and they spat it out. They ran, and they ran, and they ran. And of course, when they returned the next day to threaten and repeat their claim to a share of the crop, the barber and his clever wife just laughed at them.

"Have a care!" the robbers cried. "Twice you fooled us: once by making us dig all night, and now by feeding us on filth so that our caste is broken – a terrible thing to do! Tonight is going to be our turn."

And then another thief hid himself in the house. But the barber's wife saw him with half an eye. And when her husband asked, "What have you done with the gold? I hope you haven't put it under the pillow," she answered:

"Don't be alarmed – it's out of the house. I've hung it in the branches of the tree outside. No one will think of looking for it there."

The thief chuckled. And when the house-folk were asleep, he slipped out and told his companions. And sure enough, there it was. The captain looked up, and there he saw it among the branches.

"One of you go up and fetch it down," he ordered.

What was there was really a hornet's nest – full of brown and yellow hornets. But it looked just like a big bag.

One of the thieves climbed up the tree, but as he came close to the nest and was reaching up to take hold of it, a hornet flew out and stung him on the thigh. He clapped his hand to the spot.

"Oh, you thief!" cried the rest from below. "You're pocketing the pieces yourself. Shabby, shabby! What a mean thing to do!"

You see, it was very dark, and when the poor man clapped his hand to the place where he had been stung, they thought he was putting his hand in his pocket. He clapped his hand to the spot.

"I'm not doing anything of the kind," said the thief. "There's something that's biting me in this tree." But just at that moment, another hornet stung him in the breast. And he clapped his hand there.

"Shame, shame! We saw you do it that time — we saw you! Just you stop that at once or we'll make you!"

And they sent up another thief, and another, but they fared no better. For by this time the hornets were thoroughly roused, and they stung the poor man and his friend all over so that they kept clapping their hands here, there and everywhere.

"Shush! shush!" called the rest. "You're going to waken the whole household."

And then the captain himself came up. He was intent on getting the prize, and he went ahead of all the rest as fast as he could go, and he pulled at the bag and out came all the hornets. The robbers were stung from head to toe. They had to go to hospital for many days.

And as for the barber's clever wife and her husband, they had some peace at last. In fact, the robbers were laid up for so long a time that she began to think they were never coming back. And she stopped keeping a watch for them.

She was wrong. She was quite wrong. For one night, when she had left the window open, she was awakened by whisperings outside. She gave herself up for lost. But she wasn't going to yield without a struggle, so she seized her husband's razor. And then she stood just inside the window. And the first thief began to creep up. She waited until the tip of his nose was visible, and then, *flash!* — she sliced it off with the razor as clean as a whistle.

"Ow!" yelled the thief, "I've cut my nose!"

"Shush!" said the others. "You'll waken the household. Go on."

"Not I!" the thief said. "I'm bleeding like a pig."

"Huh! Knocked your nose against the shutter, I suppose," said the second thief. "Well, I'll go."

But *ssssh!* – off went the tip of his nose too.

"Dear me," he said. "There certainly is something sharp here."

"A bit of bamboo on the lattice," said a third thief. "I'll go..."

And *flick!* – off went his nose too.

"It's extraordinary!" he exclaimed. "It's extraordinary! I feel as if someone had cut off the tip of my nose."

"Rubbish!" said the fourth. "What cowards you all are! Let me go."

But he fared no better.

Nor the fifth thief.

Nor the sixth.

And now it was the captain's turn.

The captain was a very handsome man, and he had a particularly shapely nose. And he thought he didn't want to lose it. He said, "It won't be a good thing for all of us to be disabled. One man must continue unhurt to protect the wounded. Let us return another night." He was a cautious man, you see, and he valued his nose.

So they all crept away sulkily, and the barber's clever wife lit a lamp and gathered up all the nose tips, and she put them away safely in a little box.

Now before the robbers' noses were healed over, the hot weather set in. The barber and his wife found it warm sleeping in the house, so they put their beds outside. They made sure the thieves would not return.

But they did come back – and seizing such a good opportunity for revenge, they just took the wife, bed and all, and carried her off fast asleep.

She woke to find herself borne along on the heads of four thieves while the other three ran beside her. She gave herself up for lost. And then she thought, and she thought, and she thought, and she tried to think of some way to escape.

And then, just as luck would have it, the robbers paused for rest under a banyan tree. Quick as lightning she seized hold of a branch that was within reach, and she swung herself up into the tree, winding the bedsheet around her as she went.

"Let's rest here a bit," said the thieves. "We've plenty of time, and we're tired, and she's dreadfully heavy."

The barber's wife couldn't help laughing. But she had to keep still, for it was a bright moonlit night. And the robbers set down their burden, then began to squabble as to who should take the first watch. And at last they determined that it had to be the captain because, after all, he did not have a sore nose.

So they all went to sleep, and the captain walked up and down in the moonlight, watching the bed, and the barber's wife sat perched up in the tree and watched him.

Suddenly an idea came into her head. She began to sing softly. The robber captain looked up, and saw the veiled figure of a woman in the tree. Of course, he was a little surprised. But he was a good-looking young fellow, and very vain of his appearance, and he decided it was a fairy who had fallen in love with his handsome face. Fairies sometimes do such things, you know, especially on moonlit nights. So he twirled his great moustaches, and he strutted about waiting for her to speak.

But when she just went on singing and took no notice of him, he stopped and called, "Come down, my beauty, come down. I won't hurt you."

But she just went on singing.

So he climbed up into the tree, determined to attract her attention. When he came quite close, she turned her head away and sighed.

"What's the matter, my beauty?" he asked. "You're a fairy, aren't you? You've fallen in love with me, but there's nothing to sigh for, nothing to sigh for."

"Ah!" said the barber's wife, with another sigh. "You're fickle – I'm sure you're fickle. Men with long pointed noses like yours always are. My mother told me."

But the robber captain swore he was the most constant of men. But the fairy sighed and sighed until he wished his nose had been shortened too.

"You're telling stories, I'm sure," said the fairy. "I know – move a little closer and just let me touch your tongue with the tip of my tongue, and I'll be able to taste if you're fickle or not."

So the robber captain put out his tongue, and *snip!* – the barber's clever wife bit off the end of it.

What with the fright and the pain, he tumbled off the branch, and he fell bump on the ground. He sat with his legs very far apart, looking as if he had come from the skies.

"What is the matter?" cried his comrades, awakening to the noise of the fall.

"*Bul-ul-a-bul-ul-ul!*" he said, pointing up into the tree, for of course he couldn't speak plainly without the tip of his tongue.

"What is the matter?" they bawled in his ears, as if that would do any good.

"*Bul-ul-a-bul-ul-ul!*" he said, pointing upwards.

"The man's bewitched!" cried one. "There must be a ghost in this tree."

Just then, the barber's wife began flapping her veil and howling. Without waiting to look, the thieves set off in fright, dragging their leader with them. And the barber's clever wife climbed down from the tree, put her bed on her head, and walked quietly home.

After this the thieves saw that it was no use trying to gain their point by force, so they went to court to claim their share. But the barber's wife pleaded her case well, and she brought the noses and the tongue tip as witnesses. So the judgement went for her, and the king made the barber his chief advisor, saying he'll never do anything foolish as long as his wife is alive. And that is the story of the lazy barber's wife.

Rebirth and Return

The Blue Faience Hippopotamus

ON AN ISLAND in the Nile long ago, just up before the First Cataract, there lived a princess, the youngest daughter of a pharaoh. She had been born in the royal palace, but she'd grown very tired of that. She was young, and everybody else was old – her brothers and sisters, her father – old and stupid; unworthy to wear the Double Crown of Egypt. So she thought to herself, "I'll get a boat, and I'll travel up the river, and I'll find myself an island. I'll take my old nursemaid with me, and gardeners, and men to row, and some servants, and we'll live there. And no one will be old, and no one will be cross. And maybe a prince will come by some day, and he'll see me and marry me."

So that's what they did. They took the boat, and they went up the river till they came to the island. And they went ashore. And the gardeners began to make a garden of the island. And the nursemaid, of course, was pleased because she had her little princess to look after. And as for the men who rowed the boat, they married the maids. So everyone was very happy.

The princess used to go to the far side of the island every morning and swim. And when she had finished her swim she would lie in the sun and dry herself off. In the mud nearby there lived a young hippopotamus. And he saw her, and he loved her. He had never loved anything like this in all his life. He thought about her all day. He thought about her all night. But he was a hippopotamus, and she was a human princess.

And his friends and his family all said to him, "Stop thinking about her. Go and find yourself a nice female hippopotamus and marry her, and have lots of hippopotamus children."

And he said, "Yes, that's what I'll do." But he didn't do it – because always the vision of the little princess crept into his dreams. He didn't know what to do; he was really in despair about it.

One day he was lying there in the mud thinking about it and he heard two herons talking. One was very excited. He'd been up beyond the Third Cataract, and there he had found a magician – a wonderful magician. "He can do anything!" The heron was telling his wife. "He can do anything! He can turn giraffes into butterflies, and butterflies into gazelles – he can turn anything into anything, just at the drop of a hat!"

And she said, "Oh, you men – you men, you get so excited about things. I can turn an egg into a baby heron just by sitting on it, and who gets excited about that?" And then the two of them flew away, quarreling softly, you know, the way married people do.

But the little hippopotamus lay there in the mud, thinking and thinking and thinking. "Beyond the *Third* Cataract! I've never been as far as the Second." And he started to swim.

It was a long, long way. The days turned into weeks and the weeks turned into months and the months turned into a year, and then almost a second year. And then one day he saw ahead of him a great face of rock, and opening out of it was a cave. And as he approached the cave he saw two of the most surprised looking butterflies he had ever seen in his life.

So he stood there looking into the cave and there was an old man sitting on a pile of skins. He was weaving something. The hippopotamus stood there for a long time looking at him, and at last the man said, "Look, will you come in if you're coming in, or will you move away? You're blocking all the light." So he went in.

"Did you want something?" said the old man. "Because if you don't, don't interrupt."

"Yes," he said, "I wondered about something."

"What did you wonder about?"

"Well, I saw two butterflies coming out of here. They looked very surprised. I wondered if they had been giraffes?"

"No, not giraffes. They were gazelles. But clever of you, clever of you to notice. What could I do for you?"

"Could you change me into something?"

"What do you want to be changed into?"

"Something that a princess would love."

"Oh. Change you into a chocolate cake?"

"No, no. Could you make me a prince?"

"Not humans, no. Nothing but trouble. Why not the cake?"

"No, I don't want her to eat me, I want her to love me."

"Well, I could change you into face paint. All girls love that."

"It's not what I want," said he.

"What's wrong with what you are?"

"I'm so big."

"I suppose I could make you smaller. I could change your colour; I could change your shape. Any of those?"

"Yes," he said. "I'd like to be much, much smaller."

"What colour would you like to be?"

"Oh, blue. Blue is her favourite colour. She loves blue."

"So, you're to be smaller, and you're to be blue. What shape would you like to be?"

"Oh, my own shape. I don't really think there's any nicer shape than hippopotamus. It's just the size that's a problem."

"All right," he said. "All right."

"But... but...," said the hippopotamus, "how can I be sure I'll get to the princess?"

"I'll see to that," said the magician. "I'll see to that. There's a traveller passing by very soon. He'll take you down. I'll see that you get to the princess. But listen to me very carefully. I'll give you one wish. I always give everyone I change one wish. Because you may find you've made a mistake. If you want to go back to your old form, this wish will let you. But be careful – be very careful. Don't suddenly in a little boat say, 'I wish I was a hippopotamus again.' That would be a very bad thing to do. Wait till you're where a hippopotamus should be before you make a wish like that. Now, alright, are you ready?"

"I'm ready," said the little hippopotamus. And suddenly the walls moved back farther and farther away from him. And the ceiling – the ceiling was higher than the sky, it seemed. And what was this he was leaning against? This enormous thing like a mountain was the shoe of the magician. He had been changed.

Just at that moment, there was a cry outside and in came the merchant. He picked up those things that the magician had ready for him to take and sell, and he put them into his pack. And among them, wrapped in a piece of fine linen, was the little hippopotamus. And they went down the river. He thought of the year and the second year it had taken him to get up, and he was down in a few hours.

And they came ashore on the island, and there was the little princess. And she said, "Oh, oh, I must have that! That little blue hippopotamus. I just love him." So she bought him, and she had him. She adored him and he was with her wherever she went. And at night he was on a little table beside her bed. He was never far away from her, and she talked to him. And he loved her. And time went by.

Then suddenly the little princess was not so little any longer. She seemed less happy. Every now and again, at night, the hippopotamus would hear her crying. And one night she said to him, "Oh, little hippopotamus, aren't you lucky to have no feelings! No thoughts and feelings at all. I'm so unhappy. When I came up here I thought – I thought a boat would come by and a young prince on it and he would see me and come and marry me. But the boats go by all the time and they wave. But they never come ashore. And I'm so lonely."

Then she blew out the lamp and tried to go to sleep, and the little hippopotamus thought of his wish. He thought of the cool deep water again, and the taste of waterplants under his tongue, and the beauty of a young female hippopotamus he remembered. He thought, "If I had never seen the little princess bathing, I might have a son by now or a little daughter."

And then he thought, "Tomorrow I will use my wish and go back again to the river – the black, cool Nile."

Then he remembered the little princess and her tears. He used his one wish, and he said, "May the man who belongs to the princess's heart arrive here tomorrow and may they be happy forever."

And you know the very next day it happened. A pleasure boat came up the river, and a young prince was on it, and he saw the princess and she saw him, and they knew they would never be lonely anymore. And the whole day was full of joy and sunshine, and only one bad thing happened in it. And that was that a servant, dusting, knocked the little hippopotamus off the table where he was placed. And he broke into a hundred pieces. And the little princess wept. But then her mind was on the prince, and she went away and forgot all about it.

127

As for the little hippopotamus, the next thing he knew he woke up. And he was back in the cave of the magician.

"It's all right," said the magician. "It's all right. I arranged for you to be brought back here, and I've got all the pieces of you." He said, "You know, in all the years that I've been changing people and giving them wishes, no one before has ever used his wish for anyone else. No one. And just for that, just for that in your next life you don't have to be one of the lower animals. You can be a man. In fact, you can be the highest form of man. You can be an Egyptian."

And you know what the next words that the little hippopotamus heard were? They were in the voice he loved most in the whole world. And it said, "He's the most beautiful baby that ever was born! Oh my son, oh my little son!" And you know, she never knew. She never knew that he had once been a little blue hippopotamus.

The Silver Saucer
and the Transparent Apple

GOD KNOWS BEST, and he makes some of us wise and some of us foolish, some of us rich and some of us poor, some of us merchants and some of us fishermen. Anyway, he made this man a merchant. He had boxes and great chests and drawers, keys, and things like that. Also he had three daughters.

Two of them were beautiful enough, God knows, but the little one – oh, the little one, she was like a birch tree in the spring! She wasn't only beautiful, she was good. She did all the hard work of the house. She got up early and lit the fires. She did the cooking, she swept the floors. And for that the others called her Little Stupid. "Little Stupid, do this. Little Stupid, do that. Little Stupid, do the other thing. Little Stupid, there's dust under the rug."

One day the old father came to them and he said, "The snow will soon be here. I'm going off to town on some business. Maybe I won't be there again for a while, so if there's anything you would like me to bring you, let me know. What would you like from the great city?"

And the eldest one said, "Father, I want a dress. I want a dress of silk with a gold hem. Long – touching the floor."

And the second one said, "Father, I want a necklace. I want it of shining jewels – red and green and purple and all colours."

And the little one said, "Father, let me help you on with your coat. And have some hot soup before you go." But he said to her, "Don't you want a present, my little one?" She was his favourite, you know.

She said, "Father, if you can find them in the market, I would like a silver saucer and a transparent apple."

So the sleigh bells rang, and the old father went away. And Little Stupid dusted and swept and cooked and cleaned, and those two lazybones, they lay in bed, toasting their toes till noon every day. And then they came down and complained that the house was not hot enough, or there was dust somewhere. You know – complain, complain, complain.

And then the sleigh bells rang again, and father came back. And they ran out to the door to meet him, and the eldest said, "Father, did you get my dress?" And he gave it to her.

And the second one said, "Father, my necklace, my necklace!"

And the little one said, "Father, the fire's nice and warm, come in and get warm. I've made you some tea."

So after he had drunk his tea and she'd helped him off with his cold clothes, he gave her her present. "I had a hard time finding it," he said. "I looked all over the market for it. And then I found an old Jewish merchant who'd been in every country in the world. And he sold me the silver saucer. As for the apple, it was a Finnish woman, and her cheeks were as rosy as the apple itself. And she sold it to me. What are you going to do with it?"

And the little one, she sat down in her little chair, and she put the saucer in her lap, and she put the apple into the saucer, and she turned it round with her fingers. She turned it faster and faster and faster, till you couldn't see the saucer or the apple, just a soft blue light. And then it spread out wider and wider, and became a great soft light. And in it you could see the whole land of Holy Russia spread out before you. The great rivers flowing to the sea, the ships out on the water, the merchants in the marketplace, even children in school. And she sat there, looking and looking.

And the two sisters went and put on their fine clothes, and they looked at themselves in the mirror. And they admired themselves in the mirror. But, you know, there was nobody to be jealous of them. There was nobody to see them. There was nobody to want their things. New things get a bit tiresome if there's nobody but yourself to look at them. So after a while they came and watched the little one. And then the eldest one said to her, "I'll give you my dress for your saucer and your apple, Little Stupid."

"No, thank you, I couldn't do that."

"I'll give you my necklace."

"No, thank you, I couldn't do that."

"Give them to us," they said.

"I couldn't do that," she said. "I want my own."

So they went off, and they began to talk. And after a while they came in to her, and they said, "Come, Little Stupid, we're going out to pick berries, and you have to come."

"I don't want to," she said.

"Well, you have to," they said. "Who's going to carry the baskets if you don't come?"

"All right," she said, "but wait for me for a minute."

And she took her saucer and her apple and she went to her father, and she said, "Dear father, put these away for me."

So he said he'd put them away for her, and he locked them up in a great box and turned the key so they were safe.

And she took the baskets and they went out into the forest, and she picked berries, and she picked berries, and she picked berries till her basket was half full. But she didn't see her sisters. And after a little while she saw them coming through the forest towards her. And they had their hands behind their backs, and they were looking very strange. And she said, "Sisters, what are you doing? Your baskets aren't full. What is the matter?"

And they said, "Give us the saucer and the apple."

"No," she said, "I can't. I haven't got them with me."

"Give them to us," they said.

"No," she said. "I haven't got them with me." And then from behind their backs they brought out an axe, and they held it out before her. And she said to them, "Sisters, what is the axe for? You don't need an axe to pick berries."

"No," they said, "you don't need an axe to pick berries. Give us the saucer and the apple."

She said, "I haven't got them with me." And there in the deep forest, one of them caught her by the hair and one of them lifted the axe, and in the deep forest they killed her – all for the sake of a silver saucer and a transparent apple. And when she was dead they covered her over with earth and leaves. And then those wicked ones, oh, those wicked ones, they rubbed their eyes till they were red and they looked as if they'd been crying. And they went home through the forest and they said to their father, "We were out picking berries in the forest with our sister, and a wolf came and killed her. So, she won't need her saucer and her apple anymore, so will you give them to us please?"

But he said, "My little one, my little one that they called Little Stupid because she was so good. No, no, they're all I have now to remember her by. I'll keep them."

So you see, they didn't even get the saucer and the apple.

And the days went by, and the old man wept, and cried and cried for his Little Stupid. And the snow came and covered the ground, and the old man still cried.

And then the snow began to melt, and the old man stopped crying because, you know, the old forget. But the two sisters, they never forgot. There wasn't a single solitary day that they didn't wish for Little Stupid back. Who got up now and lit the fire in the morning? They did. Who did the cooking and the sweeping and the cleaning? They did. They would have given anything to have Little Stupid back.

Well, the snow really began to melt, and the spring came. And there was a little shepherd boy who took his sheep out into the woods, to see if he could find some fresh green grass for them. And deep, deep in the forest he came upon a clearing. And in the middle of the clearing there was a little bit of green. It looked – it looked like a tiny grave. And all around it were the first flowers of spring: yellow and blue and red. And growing up, straight up out of the middle of the little mound, there was a reed.

The little shepherd looked at it all and he thought, "That would make a good pipe, wouldn't it?" And he took his knife out of his pocket and he cut the reed, and very carefully he cut the stops in it and made a pipe, clearing out the pith from the inside. And then when it was all ready he lifted it to his lips and he said, "I wonder. I wonder what song it will play."

But you know he never found out, because before he could even think – he had just breathed in it – the pipe began to sing. And it sang in a girl's voice and it said, "In the deep forest they killed me, they killed me. All for the sake of a silver saucer and a transparent apple." And once again it sang, "In the deep forest they killed me, they killed me, all for the sake of a silver saucer and a transparent apple."

And the shepherd boy was afraid. He took the pipe and went running to town as fast as he could go. And in the middle of the little town he put it to his lips and played it again. And the people gathered round to hear, until there was a great crowd about him. And on the edge of the crowd there was an old man. When he heard what the pipe said he came forward, and there were tears streaming down his face. And he said, "I had a little daughter. They called her Little Stupid because she was so good. And she had a silver saucer and a transparent apple. Take me to where you found this."

So the little shepherd boy took him deep into the forest and they came to the little grave. And once again the little shepherd boy put the pipe to his lips. But this time it sang a different song. It sang, "Father, dear father, waken me from this cruel sleep. O my father, go up to the palace of the Tsar, the Little Father, and ask him for a cup full of water from his holy well, and come back and pour it over me, and wait."

And a few days later as the Tsar, the Little Father, came out of his palace and down the steps he found an old man waiting for him. And the old man said to him, "O great Tsar, O great Tsar, Little Father, I pray you, grant me a boon. Grant me a cup of water from the holy well."

"What for?" asked the Tsar. So the old man told him, and the Tsar said, "Take more cups than one, so that you can run fast without spilling them all. And when you've wakened your little daughter — if you waken her — bring her and let me see her. And bring the silver saucer and the transparent apple. Oh, and the little shepherd boy too, and the two sisters. Everyone."

So the old father went back deep into the forest as fast as his legs could carry him, and without spilling all the water. And they got back, and the two of them — the little shepherd boy and the old man — they knelt down by the grave, and very gently and very tenderly they cleared away the earth. And there underneath was Little Stupid, lying with her eyes closed as if she were asleep. And they poured the water over her, and she opened her eyes and sat up.

They were so happy. They got a cart though, an old farm cart, and they put her into it. And the silver saucer and the transparent apple. And the two sisters, bound with their hands together. And the little shepherd boy. And they all went up to the Tsar's palace. And the Tsar heard the whole story again. And he looked at them all, and he said, "You two wicked sisters, as soon as the sun sets you'll be taken outside the city wall and shot."

But Little Stupid said, "Oh no, oh no! They're my sisters. We were children together in our father's house. Don't shoot them. Send them home to their father."

The Tsar was pleased, he was very pleased. He sent them home to their father, telling them to be better daughters than they had been. And I wish I could tell you that they were. But they probably were not. People don't change all that much. As for the little shepherd boy, the Tsar gave him so much gold that he became a rich shepherd. And then the Tsar said to Little Stupid, "Would you stay here and marry me, and be my queen, and the Little Mother of all good Russians?"

And she asked her father, and he said of course she could. And she did. And they lived happily together and she bore him many beautiful, polite, good little children. And do you know what they played with? A silver saucer and a transparent apple. And when they grew up they had children of their own, and they had children and they had children, and they all played with them.

Perhaps at this very moment – perhaps at this very moment some descendants of those two are sitting and they're turning the apple in the saucer, and it's going round and round and round. And it turns into a soft blue light and then into a bigger light, and there spread out before them is the whole land of Russia. The ships at sea, the great rivers flowing, the farmers at work in their fields, the merchants and the cities. The children, the children almost asleep. And perhaps they say, "It's time we stopped this."

Childe Rowland

ONE DAY long and long ago Childe Rowland and his two brothers were playing ball down by a churchyard. And their sister Burd Helen leaned over the gate and watched them. And after a while it chanced that Childe Rowland kicked the ball and it went up, up, up – it went right over the church and away, till you could see it no more.

And Burd Helen laughed, and she turned and ran after the ball to bring it back to her brothers. But she took the short way. She went around the right side of the church, which is called going widdershins, and it's a very dangerous thing to do. It's against the sun, and of course with the sun in your face your shadow goes behind you, and you can't guard it. And it's a thing you should never do, but it's what she did. And the brothers waited, and they waited, and they waited. But Burd Helen did not come back.

> Long they waited, and longer still,
> And she came not back again.

Burd Helen had disappeared – she had disappeared like dew on a May morning.

137

They sought her east, they sought her west,
They sought her up and down.
But woe were the hearts of her brethren,
Since she was not to be found.

After time had gone by and she had not come back, and they could not find her, her eldest brother went to the mighty magician Merlin, and asked him what they could do.

And Merlin thought about it, and he said to him, "If she went widdershins around the church, and cast her shadow behind her, she put herself into the power of the people of Faërie, and they have probably stolen her away, shadow and all. And now if you want to find her, she is probably in the Dark Tower of the King of Elfland."

"And can anyone go there and bring her home?" asked her brother.

"It would take the bravest knight in Christendom to do it," said Merlin. "And even he might lose his life."

"If it be possible to bring her back," said the oldest brother, "I will do it, or perish in the attempt."

"Possible it is," said Merlin, "but woe to the man or the mother's son who goes without knowing what he should know, and hasn't the proper instruction."

Now the eldest brother of fair Burd Helen was brave indeed; danger and death did not dismay him. So he begged the great magician to tell him what he needed to know. And Merlin told him the things that he needed to know, and he stayed there until he had learnt them well. And then he girt his sword about him, and he said goodbye to his mother and to his two brothers, and he set off.

And long they waited, and longer still,
With muckle doubt and pain.
But woe were the hearts of his brethren,
For he came not back again.

So after a time Burd Helen's second brother went to Merlin the magician and said, "School me also, for I intend to go to find my brother and my sister in the Dark Tower of the King of Elfland and bring them back." For he also was brave indeed, and danger and death did not dismay him. And when he had been well schooled and had learned his lesson, he said goodbye to Childe Rowland and to his mother, and he girt on his sword and he set out for the Dark Tower of Elfland to bring back Burd Helen and his eldest brother.

And long they waited, and longer still,
With muckle doubt and pain.
And woe were his mother's and brother's hearts,
For he came not back again.

Now when they had waited and waited a long, long time, Childe Rowland went to his mother and besought her to let him go and seek his brothers and Burd Helen.

And at first she said no. She said to him, "You're the last of all my children, and if you were lost, all are lost and I have none left to me." But as he went on begging and begging, at last she said, "Go then. Go." And she girt on him his father's sword, the brand that never struck in vain, and she chanted the spell that gives victory. And Childe Rowland bade her goodbye, and went to the caves of the great magician Merlin.

"Once more master – once more there comes to you a pupil to be schooled. So tell me now how a man or mother's son may find the Dark Tower of the King of Elfland, and how I may bring home alive my sister and my brothers."

"My son," said the wizard Merlin, "there are two things. They are simple to tell, but hard to do. But you must learn them and remember them and do them. And they're not hard to learn. The first thing is a thing to do, and the second thing is a thing not to do. And the first thing, the thing to do, is this: when you get into the land of Faërie, and you know you're in the land of Faërie, if anyone speaks to you, you must immediately draw your sword and cut off their head. And the second thing, the thing not to do: when you get into Elfland you must bite no bite and sup no sup. For if you bite a bite or sup a sup in all the time that you are there, you will never see Middle Earth again. Never."

And Merlin bade him goodbye, and when Childe Rowland had learned his two lessons over and over till he knew them by heart, he thanked the great master and he went on his way to the Dark Tower of the King of Elfland. And he journeyed far and he journeyed fast, and at last in his journeyings he came to a great moor. And there in the moor he met a horseherd guarding his horses. And Childe Rowland looked at the horses, and their eyes were red like coals of fire, and he knew he was in Faërie. And he said to the horseherd, "Can you tell me how to get to the Dark Tower of the King of Elfland?"

And the horseherd said, "No, I cannot tell you that. But if you go away from here you will meet a cowherd, and you can ask the cowherd." And immediately Childe Rowland took his sword and he cut off the horseherd's head, and it rolled across the moor, frightening the horses. And he went on his way.

Before long he came to the cowherd, and the cowherd was on the moor, and the cows were around him. And the cows stood there, and they gazed at Childe Rowland with fiery eyes, so that he knew he was still in the land of Faërie. And he said to the cowherd, "Can you tell me how to get to the Dark Tower of the King of Elfland?"

And the cowherd said, "No, I cannot tell you. But if you go on a little way from here you will find a little woman with fowl, feeding them. She will be able to tell you." And immediately Childe Rowland drew his sword and cut off the head of the cowherd, and it rolled among the cows, frightening them. But he went on his way.

And after a little while, in a quiet place with trees, he found an old woman in a grey shawl, feeding fowl. But the fowl, as they ran around at her feet eating what she gave them, had little red eyes. And he knew that he was still in the land of Faërie. And he said to her, "Old woman, can you tell me how to get to the Dark Tower of the King of Elfland?"

And she said to him, "Oh yes, I can tell you, I can tell you. Go on a little way from here, and you will come to a low green hill, set against the blue sky. And there are three terraces in that green hill – one, and two, and three. And go around them: the first one, the second one, and the third one. Be sure to go around them widdershins. If you do not go around them widdershins, nothing will work and they will not open to you. And as you go around the first one, say *Open from within, let me in, let me in.* And as you go around the second one, say *Open wide, open wide, let me inside.* But as you go around the third terrace, say *Open fast, open fast, let me in at last.* And then a door will open, and let you into the Dark Tower of the King of Elfland. Only remember to go around it widdershins. Good luck to you."

Now the henwife spoke so fair that Childe Rowland was about to go on, and suddenly he remembered Merlin's words to him. And he drew his sword, and cut off the henwife's head.

He went on his way, and before very long he came to a low

green hill against the blue sky. And there were three terraces running around it. Then he did as the henwife told him, not forgetting to go around widdershins. And when he got to the third terrace, he said *Open fast, open fast, let me in at last.* And he saw a door which opened and let him in. Then it closed behind him with a click, and Childe Rowland was left in the dark, for he had gone at last into the Dark Tower of the King of Elfland.

It was very dark at first, perhaps because the sun had blinded his eyes. But after a while it became twilight. But where the twilight came from, there was nothing to tell him. There was no window. It must have come through the walls or through the roof. There were no candles. But in the gloaming light he could see a long passage of rough arches, and he made his way through them. And the air was warm, warm as it always is in Elfland.

He went on and on, until he found himself before two wide doors that were barred against him. But the minute he touched them, they opened before him. And he saw a wonderful, large and spacious hall that seemed to him to be as long and broad as the green hill itself. The roof was supported by pillars, wide and lofty like the pillars of a cathedral. They were of gold and silver, fretted into foliage, and between and around them were woven wreaths of flowers. And the flowers were of diamonds and rubies and topaz. And the leaves were made of emeralds. And the arches met in the middle of the roof, where hung by a golden chain an immense lamp made of a hollowed pearl, white and translucent. And in the middle of this lamp was a mighty carbuncle, blood red, that kept spinning round and round, shedding its light to the very ends of the huge hall, so that the hall seemed to be filled with the shining of the setting sun.

Now at one end of the hall was a splendid couch of velvet and silk and gold. And on it sat fair Burd Helen, combing her beautiful golden hair with a golden comb. But her face was set and wan, as if it were made of stone. And when she saw Childe Rowland she never moved, but her voice came like the voice of the dead, saying,

> *God pity you, poor luckless fool!*
> *What have you here to do?*

Now at first Childe Rowland wanted to run to her and clasp her in his arms, and just as he started to do that he remembered Merlin's words, and he drew his sword as he had been told, and turning his head away he cut off her head. And then when he dared to turn around, there she was before him. She was her own self, and joy was fighting with her fears, and she clasped him in her arms, and she cried,

> *But sit you down, my dearest dear,*
> *Oh, woe that you were born;*
> *For come the King of Elfland in,*
> *Your fortune is forlorn.*

With tears and smiles she seated him beside her on the splendid couch, and they told each other what they each had suffered and done. He told her how he had come to Elfland, and she told him how she had been carried off, shadow and all, because she ran around the church widdershins. And she told how her two brothers had been entombed, and lay as if dead, just because they did not have the courage to obey the great magician's lessons to the letter, and they had not cut off her head.

Now after a time Childe Rowland became very hungry. He had travelled far and travelled fast, and thinking that all was over, and forgetting the second command, he asked Helen to bring him food. She, still being under the spell, could not warn him. And she got up sadly, and went and brought him a bowl with bread and milk. And he took it into his hands. And he was about to eat it, but as was the custom in those days he raised it in his hands to toast her before he drank. And he met her eyes. And when he saw her eyes and the fear in them, he remembered the second command, to bite no bite and sup no sup. And he threw the bowl on the ground, and it broke. He cried then, like a challenge,

> *Not a sup will I swallow, not a bit will I bite,*
> *Till fair Burd Helen is free!*

And then immediately there came a loud roar like thunder, and a voice was heard saying,

> *Fee, fi, fo, fum,*
> *I smell the blood of a Christian man.*
> *Be he alive, or be he dead,*
> *His heart this night shall kitchen my bread!*

And then the folding doors of the vast hall burst open, and the King of Elfland entered like a storm of wind. What he was really like, Childe Rowland had not time to see, for with a bold cry Rowland answered, "Strike, sword! Strike as hard as you dare!" And he rushed to meet his foe, his good sword that never yet did fail in his hand. And Childe Rowland and the King of Elfland fought and fought. Burd Helen, with her hands clasped, watched them with fear and hope. And they fought and they fought and they fought, until at last Childe Rowland brought the King of Elfland to his knees.

"I yield me, I yield me. You have beaten me in fair fight."

And then Childe Rowland said, "I grant you mercy, I grant you mercy if you will release my sister and my brothers from all spells and enchantments; and let us go back to Middle Earth." And it was agreed.

And the Elfin King went to a golden chest where there was a vial, and the vial was full of a red liquid, ruby red. And with this liquour he anointed the ears and the eyelids, the nostrils and the lips and the fingertips of the brothers as they lay in their coffins. And immediately they sprang to life saying that their souls had only been away, but had now returned. And after this the Elfland King said a charm which took away every last bit of enchantment.

And down the huge hall that looked as if it were lit by the setting sun, and through the long passage of rough arches made of rock and all encrusted with silver, the brothers and their sister passed. And the door opened in the green hill, and it clicked behind them, and they left the Dark Tower of the King of Elfland, never to return again. For no sooner were they in the light of day than they were at home.

As for fair Burd Helen, she took care never to go widdershins around the church again.

Tattercoats

LONG AND LONG AGO, in a palace by the sea, there lived an old lord who had no kin at all except a little granddaughter whose face he had never seen. And the reason for that was because this child's birth had brought about her mother's death. At the child's birth his favorite daughter died. And when the old nurse brought the little girl to him he refused to look at her. He turned his face to the sea and he said, "Take her away. Let her live or die as she pleases. I want nothing to do with her."

And there he sat in his chair, looking out to the sea and crying. And his hair grew and grew and grew. And he grew old and the hair turned white, and it wound itself around the legs of the chair, and then it tied him to the floor so that he couldn't even move. And as for his tears, they fell big and salt down his face, and they made a little stream out of the window. And by and by the stream grew bigger and bigger, till it turned into a river, and it flowed down and joined the sea.

As for the little girl, no one cared what happened to her. She was left entirely to the servants, and they despised her. She had no clothes except rags that the old nurse found for her in the rag bag, and dressed her with as best she could. She had no shoes. She had no food except the scraps that were left around and that she picked up. The servants taunted her. They called her Tattercoats. They pushed her around. They gave her nothing of her own. And she cried and cried, and when she cried too long they threw her out of the house.

But when she was thrown out of the house she would go down to the common. And there on the common a young gooseherd tended his geese. He was an odd little boy, crippled but happy. And his geese were fat, and he played his pipe, and they danced. And when she ran down and told him all her troubles, he would play his little pipe for her until she stood up and danced with the geese and forgot all about her troubles.

And so time went on. Often the old nurse would go to the old grandfather and ask for something for the child. But he always refused. And no one else even remembered her.

Well, suddenly word began to go around that the king was travelling through the country, and his son with him. They were looking for a wife for the son. And there was to be a big ball in the town nearby, and all the great lords and ladies and their households were invited. There would be great doings that night. And the prince, if he could, would find himself a wife among them.

And when the old lord got the summons — because it was a summons — he called for the barber, and the barber came and cut him loose, and dressed his hair. And he called for the tailor and the shoemaker, and he had fine clothes made so that he could go to the ball. And the old nurse went, and asked him if he wouldn't take his granddaughter to the ball, and get her some clothes to go in. But he refused. He refused absolutely. "She's nothing to me," he said. "I have no kin."

And the nurse went back, again and again, until he ordered her out of his presence and told her to go away. And the servants said, "Ridiculous. Why should *she* go to the ball? Tatter-coats she is, and Tattercoats she should be. Her friends are geese and a gooseherd. She would never make a wife for a prince."

Sobbing bitterly, the little girl ran out of the house and down to the common, where she found the gooseherd. And he lifted his pipe to his lips and played to her. And he said, "Why do you want to go?"

And she said, "I want to see all the doings. I want to see all the things that are going on."

Then the gooseherd said to her that they should go to the castle anyway and see all the fine goings-on. But she looked at her rags and her bare feet, and she was ashamed to go. The gooseherd played a few notes on his pipe and soon she forgot all about her troubles, and the gooseherd took her by the hand and all of them set off together down the road to town: Tattercoats and the gooseherd *and* the geese.

Now, as they went along, a handsome man came riding up and asked the way to the castle where the king was lodged that night. And when he found that they were going there too, he said, "You seem merry folk. I'll get off my horse and walk too, for you seem like good company."

"Good company indeed!" said the gooseherd, and he began to play a new tune that was not dance music. It was a strange little tune, and it made the young man stare and stare at Tattercoats — not at her rags and her bare legs but at her own face.

And suddenly he said, "You are the most beautiful maiden in the world. Will you marry me?"

Yes, it was a strange tune, and the young man stared and stared at Tattercoats as if he couldn't take his eyes off her, and then again he said, "You are the loveliest maiden in the world. Will you marry me?"

The gooseherd smiled and went on playing, but Tattercoats laughed.

"Not I!" she said. "Wouldn't you be ashamed? Marrying a goosegirl without even a pair of shoes to her name?"

He asked her again, but she still said, "Go and ask one of the great ladies at the ball tonight, and don't tease poor Tattercoats."

Then he said to her, "Look, come tonight to the castle and see all the goings-on at the ball, and I promise you that I'll kiss you there *three times* before them all – the lords and ladies and the king himself."

So that night the gooseherd asked her to come to the ball, but she did not want to. "Take fortune when it comes, little one!" the gooseherd said.

And when the castle hall was full of lights and music, and all the fine company was there, and the king himself – just as the clock struck twelve – down the great ballroom came Tattercoats and the gooseherd followed by a flock of noisy, hissing geese. And the lords and ladies laughed, and the king stared in amazement.

Then the prince rose and he kissed her, before them all, three times as he had promised, and turned to the king. "Father," he said, "I have chosen my bride, and here she is, the loveliest girl in all the land."

Then the gooseherd played still another tune like a sweet bird singing, and suddenly Tattercoats' rags were shining robes, and a golden crown was on her shining head, and the flock of noisy geese little pages bearing her train, and the trumpets sounded, and the king rose to greet his new daughter-in-law.

But the old lord went home to his palace by the sea, and he sits there weeping until his tears run down in a great river to the ocean. As for the gooseherd, he was never seen again.

The Girl Who Took a Snake
for a Husband

ONCE LONG AND LONG AGO, in a land over rivers and mountains, there was a king who had three daughters. Now in that country there was a custom that on one day of every year, all the young men who were of marriageable age but were not yet married would go out and walk up and down the streets, while the young maidens who were of marriageable age but were not yet married would go up onto their rooftops, each one with a ball in her hand marked with her own name. Each girl would throw her ball, and if she hit a young man, the young man that she hit was to be her future husband. This was the law for rich and poor alike and everyone must obey it.

And so on one day of the year the three daughters of the king went up to their rooftops, each holding in her hand a ball with her name upon it. And the first one threw her ball and she hit a captain in the king's guard. And that was a suitable husband for her, and the king would be pleased. The second threw her ball and she hit a bey's son, and that was an even more suitable husband. And then the third one, the little Princess Lukja, the youngest, threw her ball, and it fell into a peasant's cart, among the vegetables. And it hit a great, spotted snake that was curled up there.

And so, when the affair was over, the soldiers brought to the king the husbands that his daughters had won for themselves. And he was very pleased with the captain in the king's guard, and he was pleased with the bey's son. But when he saw the spotted snake he said, "Take it away, take it away! This is ridiculous. Don't bring that monster into my presence."

But they said to him, "Lord, it is the law. And it applies to peasant and king's daughter alike. The Princess Lukja must either marry the snake or she will lose her life."

And then the Princess Lukja, who saw her father's distress, came to him and she said, "My father, do not be afraid. I am not afraid. I will do whatever needs to be done. But my father, first, I pray you, let me go out into the deep forest and see the wise woman there, who was my nurse when I was a child, and ask her advice about what I should do."

So they let her go, and she went out into the forest and came to the wise woman and told her her tale. And for a moment the wise woman looked distressed. But then — then she took some milk and put it in a saucer and she warmed it, and she scattered herbs into it and set it in the hands of the princess. And she looked into it for a long time and then she said, "Princess, this is better than I had thought. Do not fear, do not fear at all. Only go home and find your snake, and count carefully the number of scales on his back. And then come to me and tell me."

So she went home and she found the snake, and she counted the scales on his back, and she went back to the wise woman and she said, "There are forty scales on the back of the snake."

She said, "Listen, listen carefully. Go to your father and tell him that you will marry the snake, and that you are not afraid.

But that you would like for a wedding dress, not one wedding dress but forty. Forty thin dresses. And on your wedding day wear them, one over the other. And when the wedding feast is over, go back to your house and say to the snake, 'Is it not hot in here? I pray you, take off a scale and I will take off a dress.' And so do, until he has taken off all the scales and you have taken all the wedding dresses off."

So she went back to her father and she told him, and he set the wedding day for all three princesses. And he built a little house within the palace grounds for the Princess Lukja and her snake husband. And the wedding was celebrated as always, and there were gifts — gifts from everyone. And then they sat and feasted at a great high table. And the two elder sisters sat with their husbands beside them, and the youngest princess sat with her husband beside her in a basket. And everyone tittered and laughed.

And then the presents that had been given were opened. And three princesses stood up one by one and thanked their friends for the gifts that they had been given. And the two sisters had given to the Princess Lukja for a wedding present, a man's suit — a man's suit of scarlet cloth. And a pair of little shoes of scarlet leather.

When she had opened these the princess stood up, and prettily as a princess should she thanked everyone, and her sisters, for their gifts. And then she went home with her husband, across the courtyard to the house where they lived, the princess walking with her head high like a princess, and her husband following her, *sdrouk, sdrouk, sdrouk,* across the cobblestones.

They went into the little house and she shut the door behind them, and she sighed and she said, "My lord, is it not hot in here? Would you not like to remove a scale, and I will take off one of my dresses?" So he took off a scale and she took off a dress. And he took off another scale and she took off another dress. And so it was, till he had taken off all the scales, and she had taken off all her dresses.

And there stood before her not a snake, but the most handsome prince she had ever seen, and his snake scales in the basket. And he said to her, "I will be like this always in the night, without my snake scales, when nobody can see me, but I pray you tell nobody. Tell nobody. And take care of my snake scales. Let no harm come to them when I'm not wearing them." And she promised that she would. And they passed the night in great happiness.

And in the morning her mother came across the courtyard, knocking anxiously about the door to see how her daughter had fared during the night. And when the Princess Lukja opened the door her face was radiant, and her mother could not believe it.

And the days went by, the weeks, the months, and at last a year had passed. And the king decided that he would give a great feast to celebrate the anniversary of his daughters' marriage. So a great feast was given and guests were invited from all over the kingdom, and a band played, and there was rich food set out. And everything was very fine.

And the Princess Lukja went to the ball. She went all by herself, leaving her husband behind in his basket. The two other sisters danced and made merry, and every little while they threw glances over their shoulders at their sister as she sat in a chair by herself. And back in the little house the snake thought to himself, "How is my darling faring? I will go and see."

So he took off his snake skins and laid them away carefully, and then he looked about for something to wear. And the only thing that he could find was the little suit that had been given for a wedding present, and the scarlet shoes. And he pulled them on, and he walked across, and he looked into the room where the ball was being held. And everyone was dancing and making merry, except Princess Lukja. She sat by herself as a married woman should, for her husband was not there.

He went in and he went up to her, and he took her to dance with him. And they danced together with great pleasure, until people began to notice that he was there. And then the sisters – the sisters were very angry. "Look at her," they said, "look at her! Is it not a shame? There she is, a married woman – dancing! Dancing with a stranger. And look – look at the suit he is wearing. Look at the shoes he is wearing. Where did he get those?"

And as soon as they thought of it they left the ballroom and ran across to the little cottage, and they opened the door and went in. And there they saw the snake scales, and the snake not in his basket. And they said, "He is a magician. He is some kind of a wicked wizard. We must burn the snake scales and save her from this devil." So they set fire to the snake scales. They set fire to the snake scales. And then they turned and came back to the ball.

And the snake husband was dancing with his princess, and he suddenly said to her, "I feel faint, I feel hot, I feel dizzy. Let us go out into the garden." So they went out into the garden, and they sat there together on the stone bench, and after a while he said to her, "My love, go back to the house and see if something has happened to my snake scales."

She went back to the house, and she found the snake scales, burned away in the fire. And she came rushing back to her husband to ask him what she should do, but there was nothing on the bench but a pair of little scarlet shoes and a man's suit, folded. And she cried and cried as if her heart would break. And she didn't know what to do.

On the third day, when she could cry no longer, she went out into the forest, and she told the wise woman what had happened. And the wise woman looked at her. And she said, "Long ago, long ago when I looked in your hand, I knew who your husband was. He is the son, the cherished son, of the King of the Underworld, who wears, sometimes, the form of a snake. And all his servants are in the uniform of a snake. And his son wanted to come up into the world, but the father did not want him to, for fear he would stay and not come home. For fear he would marry a girl of this world. So he made him come in the form of a snake, and not let anyone know who he was. And now that he can no longer go back to his snake scales, he has had to go back to his father in the Kingdom of the Underworld."

And the girl said, "I will go after him, I will find him!"

But she said, "It's a long, difficult way. It's fraught with many, many dangers. You would have to go through the Moving Mountains, which open only once a day at noon with a *bumbullím* like thunder. And you must rush through the minute that they are open, before they close upon you. And then you would have to pass the cottage where dwells an evil witch – a very evil witch. And she will not let you pass unless you do service for her. And if she offers you any reward you must take from her only that which is of little value. No gold, no jewels, nothing. And you must go on till you find your way to the Snake Kingdom, and you must not be afraid. And many things will come to frighten you."

"Look," she said, "go home, and go through the ashes. Sift them carefully with your fingers, and see if you can find any, any at all, of the snake scales left. Bring them back to me."

So she went, and she found one whole snake scale that had not been burned, and a little bit of another. And she carried them back to the old woman, who sewed them into a little bag and tied it with a string, and put it around her neck. And she said, "If you must go, take this as a talisman. But it is a long and dangerous journey."

"Nothing," she said "is too long or too dangerous for me. For the only thing I care about is to find my husband."

And the next day she set off. And she walked and she walked till she came almost to the edge of the world. And there before her were the Moving Mountains. And she waited till it was almost noon, and she moved up to them. And they opened before her with a *bumbullím* like thunder, and she ran quickly through. And she was in the Underworld.

There it is different from here. The colours are different. The grass is not green. The grass is red; the skies are dark. And before her, as she looked, she saw a little cottage — a little cottage that had neither door nor window, but a great sloping roof. And she knew that she could not pass that cottage without encountering the witch.

So she went up, and she knocked upon the wall of the house. And after a while there was a sound and she looked up, and there on the roof was a great witch, a *shtríga* — the grandmother of all the witches — crawling down the roof like a bat. And the old woman said to the princess in a cracked voice, "Who are you and what do you want?"

"I want to pass, please. I want to pass your cottage and go on my way. And I would like a drink of water for I am very, very thirsty."

"Water — you shall have water," said the old witch. "Go to the well and get yourself a glass and drink it." So she went to the well and she got herself a glass of water. It was green. Little white worms crawled about in it. It was horrid. But she swallowed it down somehow, with the old woman watching her. And then the witch said, "Was it good, was it good?"

"It was sweet, it was beautiful," she said.

"Have some more!"

"No, thank you, that is all I can drink at the moment," said the princess.

"Then," said the old woman, "you want to pass, do you? You'll have to do three tasks for me."

"Anything, anything, little mother. Anything that I can do."

"Well," she said, "the first task is this. I want you to go and get my pig with the silver bristles and shut him up in his pen where he should be."

So she went down and looked for the pig with the silver bristles, and there he was. And he wasn't really hard to get. But just as she was about to shut him into the pen, down from the sky flew great black birds, and they started to attack her. And she moved this way and she moved that. She was afraid, and she didn't know what to do. She pressed the little bag which she wore around her neck. And the minute she did so, with a terrible scream the birds turned and flew away, back into the skies again. And she shut the pig into its pen and she came safely home.

And the old woman was surprised to see her, and she said, "You've come back? Have you looked after the pig?"

"Oh yes, little mother, I have."

"Well, you've done your task. Tell me, would you like a nice golden bracelet? I'll give you a nice golden bracelet to wear on your wrist."

"Oh no, mother, thank you. I'm too young to wear gold. Much too young. Please give me instead three bristles. Three bristles from the pig."

"Oh, all right," said the old woman. "Take them, then, take them. But you could have the golden bracelet."

"Have you another task for me?" she said.

"Oh yes, oh yes, I have indeed. I want you to go and collect the eggs from my hens. Collect the eggs from my golden hens, and bring them home to me."

So she went down and she found the hens. But as she started to collect the eggs, the great black birds came back again and they attacked her right and left. But this time she knew what to do and she pressed her hand to the little bag, and they flew away. And she held the eggs close to her, and she came home.

And this time the woman was even more surprised to see her. And this time she said, "You shall have a necklace. You shall have a necklace with diamonds that drop from it like dew."

"Oh no, mother, not diamonds, please. I'm too young for diamonds. Give me instead, if you please – give me instead one egg. One egg from your hens."

"All right, take it," said the old woman. "Take it. Then go and milk my wild mare."

She took the egg and she put it carefully away in her pocket, and because dark was coming on she went down to milk the wild mare quickly. She got the milk, she put it into a bowl, and she started to come home when down from the sky swooped the great black birds. And she turned this way and turned that, trying not to spill the milk. And then she pressed her hand against the little bag and the birds flew away again.

And the old woman said to her, "You've done all the tasks. What shall I give you for this one? A circlet of gold and jewels for your head? That would be pretty, wouldn't it?"

"Mother, I'm too young. Mother, give me instead what I would most like. Give me a little bottle of milk from the wild mare."

"Take it," said the old woman, "take it."

"And then can I pass?" she said.

"Not tonight. The dark's coming on. Take your milk and come — you'll sleep with me tonight."

When she had taken the milk, the old woman caught her. She dragged her up the rooftop, and she dropped her down the chimney. And Lukja found herself in a little mean room, where there was a bed on the floor where the *shtríga* slept. The woman ate her supper; she threw the bones all around. She offered the girl some food, but it was mostly bones, and she couldn't eat them. So she lay on her back in bed, and the old woman lay down on her bed and began to snore like an ox.

So it was all night. The girl didn't dare to sleep. She lay there listening. And towards morning she heard the old witch begin to stir. And the witch said, "I didn't mean to. I didn't mean to eat her. But I'm hungry! And I will." And she began to crawl across the floor.

And the girl lay there. She tried to pray but she couldn't think of a prayer, and she clasped her hands together upon her breast. And she pressed the little bag with all her might. And suddenly the old woman gave the most terrible cry, and she fled up the chimney and was gone. And she didn't see her again.

By and by she collected her milk, her bristles, and the hen's egg, and she looked for a way to get up. And painfully she crawled up the wall and out of the chimney. And she started off on her journey. She walked, and she walked, and she met with many alarming sights. And she had many trials and troubles but always, always the little bag came to her aid. And at last, suddenly, she realized she was in the country of the King of the Underworld, because all the people there were in his livery, with the snakeskins on. All were polite and kind to her, and they helped her upon her way. And she went till she came to the palace of the king.

But as she got into the great city where the palace was,

everyone was in mourning. The flags were flown low. The bells tolled a dirge, and the people wept. And she said to the guards at the palace gate, "Why is everyone so unhappy?"

And they said to her, "Oh, trouble, the most terrible trouble, has fallen upon us! The greatest trouble we have ever known! First of all, our king is deaf. And he can't hear a word, and though his counsellors come and shout in his ear, he doesn't hear a word that they say. And second, our queen that we all love, our queen has become dumb — she can't speak. She can't speak at all; she can't make any sound. And those are bad enough, but the worst of all is — the worst of all is our young prince. He went away and left us for a while, and he has come back to his own country, and he is at death's door. He is blind — he can't see. He can't see a thing."

"Well," she said, "is there nothing that would cure them?"

"No," they said, "nothing, nothing. The way to cure the king's deafness is to take ashes from the bristles, the silver bristles of the wild boar, and spread them upon his ears. The way to cure the queen is to give her an egg to eat, from a golden hen. And there is no way at all to help the young Prince, but to bathe his eyes with the milk of a wild mare. And none of these things are in our country, or any other country that we know of."

"Could you let me in?" she said. They let her in. They took her into the room where the king was sitting, and his counsellors all around him, shouting and screaming and gesticulating at him. But he just shook his head. He couldn't hear.

She said, "Bring me a little brazier." And they brought her a little brazier and she lighted it, and she laid the bristles upon it. And when they were ashes she went up to the king and very gently she rubbed his ears with the ashes.

And he looked up and he said, "I hear a man talking. I hear a cock crowing. I hear a fly crawling upon the wall."

Then they brought in the queen. The queen tried to speak, and she realized that the king's hearing had come back, and she was pleased, but she could speak not at all to show her joy.

And the princess said, "Bring me boiling water." And they brought her boiling water, and she boiled the egg in it, and she took off the top and she went to feed it to the queen. And when she had eaten a little bit she crowed like a cock. When she had eaten another little bit she clucked like a hen. But when she had eaten the whole egg, she spoke in her own sweet voice. And they were so happy they didn't know what to do.

But the king turned to her and said, "If only you could help our young prince, there is nothing in the world we wouldn't do for you."

They brought the young prince in, and the minute she saw him she knew he was her own true love. He looked but he couldn't see her, for he was blind. She went up to him, and very gently she took the little bottle of milk and she bathed his eyes.

And he said, "I see my father." And she bathed him again. And he said, "I see my mother." And she bathed him again, and he said, "I see my own true love, the Princess Lukja."

And then the king said to her, "What can we do for you?" And she told him she wanted only the one thing. She wanted her husband. And so it was agreed. And after she stayed there at the palace and was treated with every kindness, she took her husband by the hand and they went back to her own country again.

They passed the little cottage, but nobody tried to harm them because of the power of the Serpent King. And they came to the mountains, and they waited till noon and ran through, the two of them, when they opened with the *bumbullím* like thunder. And they went back to the palace of her father, and he was so glad to see them and to realize that all their troubles were over. And he said, "I'm old, and I'm weary of my crown." And he made the Princess Lukja's husband king in his place. And they ruled wisely, well and happily, all their lives long.

Epilogue: *A Sword of Power, a Mother's Blessing*

NOW THAT I AM ELDERLY, I plan my time carefully. Some years ago, when I was invited to Vancouver to participate in a weekend conference, I purposefully set my alarm for 5:00 AM each morning, so that I could take a walk along the sea wall.

On the first day, I got up, slipped into some clothes and hurried to the task. Ahead of me the moon, all rosy pink, was sinking into the water. Behind me the sky was brightening for the sunrise. It was very quiet; a few gulls cried, and smaller birds cheeped excitedly. Here and there young people, singly or in pairs, spread their mats on the shore and looked out to sea in an age-old morning ritual. There were tiny daisies in the grass and whin blossoms in the hedges. A heron stood silently on a rock. I was reminded of my childhood: the smell of the sea, familiar small flowers, an engulfing calm and peace. I found myself chanting as I had long, long ago,

> The herons on Bo Island
> Stand solemnly all day.
> Like lean old men together,
> They hunch their shoulders grey.

I wish I could get near them
And hear the things they say.

When a turn in the road brought a whole new view before me, I realized I'd better turn back. On the way, I picked up a morning paper and over orange juice, coffee, and toast, read about the state of the world. There was a pleasant review of a new children's book, but apart from that, the usual desperate story of mankind — war and death in the Near East, trouble in Ulster, battered women, weary refugees.

Gone, for me, were the herons and daisies, the rosy moon, the clean sea smell. Instead, I was faced with the world as it is — and the cry, "Someone should do something about it!"

Indeed, someone should! But who? In the fairy tales that I have loved all my life, that Someone is always the most unlikely person. Sometimes it is a gentle, ill-used young girl with a kind heart. Sometimes it is the despised and carefree youngest son of whom little is expected. Sometimes it is an old hag on a hillside or a poor beggar hoping for his dinner.

On that September Saturday, I told myself: "Why not you? You're unlikely enough!"

The next question, of course, is, "What can anyone do?" There are as many answers as there are people. Some march in parades against certain issues. Some march in parades *for* certain issues. Some hold meetings. Some speak gently to those they love. Each of us, all of us, must come to terms with the state of our world and, if we can't do anything about it, we can at least face it bravely and do the best we can with our fate.

"All right," I said to myself, "you can do it if Billy Beg could and Aschenputtel could. But they had charms of some kind: a talisman, a little twisted stick, a sword of power, a dead mother's blessing. These things made all the difference. They convinced weak and inferior beings that they could accomplish great things in spite of their size and their shortcomings."

On the way to the meeting, I kept thinking about it. The world, in spite of its beauty of sea, sky, and blossom, has always been prey to greed and war and disaster, deserved and undeserved. Where have human beings found the means to face it all? Doggedly I said, "The fairy tale is true: if you accept the situation, you conquer it."

Suppose one had a little twisted stick, a fairy transformation, a sword of power, a dead mother's blessing; what would it be like, this shining talisman that would change everything? Suddenly I knew. I'd had it all the time. But possession isn't enough; it has to be recognized, accepted, and used.

What is it? It is myth! It is the whole background of story and song poured down upon us by those who have gone before. It is reassurance and courage, a great shining that transforms dark truth into victory. Myth tells us it has all happened before and that we can pass the stories on.

> *Who does not remember the old tales?*
> *Fingers of firelight on the wall, lances of sleet*
> > *on the shutter.*
> *Whoever does not remember the old tales*
> *Has lost the key that opens the door of life.*

Patrick Kavanagh, the Irish poet, claims that unless each poet finds his personal myth, his work will degenerate:

> *... I grew*
> *Uncultivated and now the soil turns sour,*
> *Needs to be revived by a power*
> > *not my own,*

Heroes enormous who do astounding deeds
Out of this world.

What then is the myth that puts confidence into the hearts of the young and the old and the nonachiever? It is really the body of wisdom, tale, and song and sayings of those who went before us.

Today we are inclined to despise the ghetto. Our emphasis is on multiculturalism. Yet the close, confined, exclusive teaching of one's own people is very powerful: I think of it as I remember Yaffa Eliach telling her "Tales of the Holocaust," and I am haunted (and feel that strong sword in my hand) as the young boy in the concentration camp line recognizes that the strong figure behind him is none other than Elijah.

I think of it as Ron Evans, the Métis storyteller, with tears pouring down his face, tells the tale of Louis Riel. I heard it as Helen Armstrong told "The Story of Olaf," and I knew that Olaf, like Elijah, would appear when he was needed.

I hear it when the greedy and proud are put down and the meek inherit the earth.

When I came to the end of my own story on that Saturday morning, it was staring me in the face. Lugh, the son of Cian Mac Cecht and Balor's daughter, has come back, as he promised, to Ireland, which he has not seen since he was a baby.

The land is in a sorry state. The Fomorians have overrun it and the De Danaans serve them as slaves, carrying their wood and water, and cowering in fear.

Lugh comes in the evening to the king's dun where a handful of De Danaans have gathered. He is allowed in because he can prove his power as an *ildánach*, a master craftsman. After demonstrating various skills and playing chess with the king, he lifts the great harp that belongs to the Dagda and plays it.

He plays the music of joy, and outside the dun the sad little company hear the birds sing, and they have never known such gladness. He plays the music of sorrow, and the De Danaans weep. They have never wept for any grief.

He plays the music of peace, and outside the snow falls softly. The De Danaans sleep while Lugh steals away, back to his young companions. It is morning when they wake. Lugh is gone. Their situation is unchanged. They are still a conquered people, broken in spirit, and the Fomorians still rule the land.

But something is different. They are suddenly refreshed, for they have heard the proud song of the harp.

And the king said, "The Fomorians have not taken the sun out of the sky. Let us go to the Hill of Usna and send to our scattered comrades, that we may make a stand."

If we have myth, we have our shining talisman. We are not alone, for behind us are those who told tales before us, and waiting are the generations to come.

And we carry, each one of us, a sword of power and a mother's blessing.

Notes

by Sean Kane

"I love telling the wondertale," Alice Kane remarked when the idea of publishing a collection of her favourite stories was suggested to her. "That is what I have done all my life, what the children I worked with liked, and what my kind of storytelling is." The wondertales — "those longish fairy tales," as she describes them, "that have elements in them sometimes of myth, at other times of simple folktale, and always of enchantment" — have been her specialty ever since she began telling stories as a children's librarian in the 1930s. This collection brings together seventeen of her favourite wondertales. They are among the best a storyteller has found in sixty years of telling.

The stories were taped during performances and, when they were typed, were presented to Miss Kane, who made some changes before approving them. But her approval did not come readily. This was the first time she had ever seen any of her stories in type, and it was a terrifying experience for her. She had never imagined that these were in any sense *her* stories. In her mind, they belonged to the authors whose books she had originally learned them from. And then, she was shocked to discover that over the years she has told and retold the stories, she has changed them in many small ways. This bothered her greatly because she has a faithful memory, and because it had been part of her training as a children's librarian to tell a story word for word, as the person who wrote the story down intended. "I worked very hard to choose versions I liked," she said. "And then I worked even harder to learn those versions in the way the author of my choice wrote them."

But that was thirty, forty – in some cases, sixty years ago. And it takes the fraction of a second for the narrative imagination to play tricks on even the most faithful memory. "I always *felt* it was exact," Miss Kane declared – and her version was: it was true to the *spirit* of the story, to a pattern of meaning and delight that had kept the story alive for generations and generations. To the storyteller, these are not old stories found in old books: they are the way life happens, and so the version told will differ from the one originally heard or read. The version may not even be the same as the one the storyteller last told. That is why several tapings of a story, performed on separate occasions before different audiences, had to be compared in order to arrive at the most expressive telling for this collection. The story is reborn in the chancy, fragile magic of its telling, the moments when it truly exists. Nevertheless, Alice Kane speaks of her debt to the beautiful books which stand behind her art, and the authors and artists of the golden age of the literary wondertale, who carried the oral tradition through a dark time.

The Dreamer Awakes was made with the assistance of friends of Alice Kane. I thank them on her behalf, for their advice and help: Johanna Hiemstra, Robert Bringhurst, Karen Denis, David Jaeger, Margaret Johnston, Kelly Liberty, Bella Pomer, Ruth Stedman, Tish Woodley, and Dan Yashinsky. Kate Stevens furnished the information for the note about "The Peach-Blossom Forest." Margaret Poynton assisted with the editing of "The Seven Wild Geese." The author and I also thank Margaret Crawford Maloney and the staff of the Osborne and Lillian H. Smith Collections of Early Children's Books in the Toronto Public Library. And we are especially grateful to Nicole Hallett, who transcribed the stories from their oral form and helped prepare the manuscript for publication.

The verse which gives the title to *The Dreamer Awakes* is an eastern European storytelling formula. Alice Kane often recites a version found at the end of some of the tales. The version printed here, which serves better as an epigraph, was heard by Robert Bringhurst in Romania.

Ivon Tortik

This Breton story has long been associated with Alice Kane, who says: "It has many charms for me: its liveliness and humour, its setting among the orchards and windmills and heather-covered moors of Brittany, and the tall stones – the dolmens – familiar to me in childhood. Long ago when I was a young children's librarian, I found on the library shelves a dull blue book with silver trim and stylized drawings called *Three and the Moon*. It was a collection of fairy tales translated from the old French. The first story in the book had been familiar to me all my life as an Irish story, with its refrain:

> *Monday, Tuesday;*
> *Monday, Tuesday;*
> *Monday, Tuesday and Wednesday . . .*

I have been telling 'Ivon Tortik' for fifty years and I have only once again in all that time seen the book it came from. I never tell the story without a burst of gratitude to its collector and translator whose name is Dorey."

In its full title, the story is "Ivon the Twisted and the Daughter of the Pleumeur Miller," in Jacques Dorey, *Three and the Moon: Legendary Stories of Old Brittany, Normandy and Provence* (1929). Dorey weaves together in this tale motifs found in the first collection of the folksongs of the Breton people, made by Théodore Hersart, vicomte de la Villemarqué: *Barzas-Breiz: Chants populaires de la Bretagne* (1839).

The Tale of the Tsar Saltan and Prince Guidon

A *skazka* in the real poetic manner of Russia, this story has all the features of the Russian wondertale: an inexhaustible flow of marvels, a forward-moving pace, splendent images – all happening as fast as language allows. Here is a swan who speaks the language of Old Russia, a young prince who is growing by the minute, envious sisters, a magic squirrel, and a city in the midst of the blue sea-ocean. The source of the retelling is Ida Zeitlin, *Skazki: Tales and Legends of Old Russia*, illustrated by Theodore Nadejan (1926). The tale was made known throughout Europe by Aleksandr Pushkin's verse narrative *The Tale of Tsar Saltan, of his Son, the Glorious and Mighty Knight, Prince Guidon, and of the Fair Swan-Princess*, illustrated in 1905 by the great Russian artist Ivan Yakovlevich Bilibin (1876–1942).

The Golden Apples of Lough Erne

This is a retelling of a story collected by the Irish poet William Butler Yeats (1865–1939), and it can be found in the Modern Library edition of his *Irish Folk and Fairy Tales* as "The Story of Conn-eda." About collecting folklore, Yeats says in the introduction to this book: "You must go adroitly to work, and make friends with the children, and the old men.... The old women are most learned, but will not so readily be got to talk, for the fairies are very secretive, and much resent being talked of." In fact, Yeats, who was not fluent in Irish, relied more for his collecting on the efforts of friends, and on the back issues of scholarly magazines like the *Cambrian Journal*, where he found this tale, published in 1855. Told in Irish by the storyteller Abraham M'Coy, it had been translated into the sophisticated literary English favoured by collectors at a time when Irish was thought to be vulgar. Here it is retold with the oral directness and simplicity that was heard for the first time in the collections made just after the publication of Yeats's influential *Fairy and Folk Tales of the Irish Peasantry* (1888).

The horse in this tale is a druid horse. The Firbolgs or "bagmen" are, according to legend, the older and more sinister of the two Faërie races. Short and spiteful, and carrying their bags (*boilg*) on their bellies like sporrans, they dwell in the lakes of Ireland where they were said to have been driven by the new Bronze Age worshippers of the goddess Dana.

The Woman of the Sea

Stories of *selkies* and people who are part seal are familiar throughout the Celtic coast lands, and Scotland, Ireland and Wales have family names whose bearers claim a seal in their ancestry. It is easy to imagine this totemic association. In *The People of the Sea: A Journey in Search of the Seal Legends* (1954), David Thomson writes: "Walk on their lonely beaches, climb on their rocks with the knowledge that ... for thousands of years people believed what you now feel – that you are at the uttermost edge of the Earth, and when all is quiet except for waves and sea birds you hear an old man gasp. You turn towards the sound. It is a seal which has broken the surface of the water to take breath, and very often seeing you it will raise its whole torso and stare back at you ... then disappear silently" (p 13).

This story follows closely "The Woman of the Sea," by the Classics scholar Helen Waddell (1889–1965) in *The Princess Splendour and Other Stories*, edited by Eileen Coldwell, illustrated by Anne Knight (1969). Waddell based her story on "The Mermaid Wife," collected originally by Thomas Keightley (1789–1872) in *The Fairy Mythology, Illustrative of the Romance and Superstition of Various Countries* (1833).

Alice Kane says of this story of the Shetlands: "Of all the English retellings, I have found none to equal Helen Waddell's in its grace and simplicity. Helen Waddell is my countrywoman. I can hear the language of Ulster in everything she writes, and in this story I can hear the soft sounds of that island evening, feel the little breeze blow up from the sea – the children's voices echoing, the smell of the hay, the bread. It brings my whole youth back to me. For me, the way to tell this story is not to liven it up in any respect. *Simplicity, Sincerity, Service*: that was the motto of the school I went to as a little girl. It applies especially to the telling of this story with its lament of the sadness of long ago."

Alice Kane is grateful to Mary M. Martin, the niece of Helen Waddell, for giving this story to the collection.

The Seven Wild Geese

The Irish poet Pádraic Colum (1881–1972) was also a student of folklore and mythology, and a noted storyteller. All his writing has the rhythm of the spoken tale that lingers in the memory. To lovers of fairy tale, his book *The King of Ireland's Son*, illustrated by Willy Pogány (1916), is full of the polyphony of oral culture. It is a collection of twenty or more Irish folk and fairy tales all woven into one continuous story happening to one young prince and his half brothers. "The Seven Wild Geese" is the title I have given to a sub-story told by one of the characters in a book where the ending of a story is found hidden among several other stories. The reader can only resolve Sheen's story by opening onto another. However, in its basic pattern the story is a complete wondertale. It is familiar in the Grimm retelling as "The Six Swans" and in the Norwegian collection by Asbjørnsen and Moe as "The Twelve Wild Ducks." Hans Andersen retells the story also. It became "The Twelve Wild Geese" in Ireland, and is one of the childhood stories heard by the Dublin bookseller Patrick Kennedy, who published it in his *Fireside Tales of Ireland* (1870).

The spaewoman is the old fortune-telling woman at the edge of town to whom everyone brings their problems. In other cultures she would be named a witch. But here she is a druidess disguised as a peasant storyteller – and not just a druidess, but Grania, the Reconciler of the Gods. Birds, especially the corncrake and the barnacle goose, are sacred to her.

Alice Kane is grateful to Máire Colum O'Sullivan for permission to retell the story.

The Korrigan

Changeling stories are especially common in the original Gaelic-speaking parts of Western Europe, where they are superstitious tales existing in the shadow of Celtic myth. If you think too highly of your child, the Otherworld may want it. The Otherworld is forever playing trick-or-treat with this one, and often you have to trick the fairies to get your own back – but you should do no more than threaten the strange child: otherwise, the fairies will do to your child what you have done to theirs.

In "The Brewery of Egg-Shells," a story collected by the British Admiralty official Thomas Crofton Croker (1798–1854) on his walking tour of Ireland and published in *Fairy Tales and Legends of the South of Ireland*, (3 vols, 1825–28), the changeling is an ominous, deep-voiced fairy. It is a *poulpican*, a witch's dwarf, in the Breton version told by Barbara Leonie Picard as "The Korrigan" in *French Legends, Tales and Fairy Stories*, illustrated by Joan Kiddell-Monroe (1955, reissued 1994). Alice Kane's version is adapted chiefly from Picard, with the "acorn before oak" verses recited as they are found in Irish retellings.

"Acorn before oak I knew" is an ancient mythological saying, probably going back to Druid tree worship. In his 12th-century "Life of Merlin," Geoffrey of Monmouth has the druidical magician say, "There is in this forest an oak laden with years. ... I saw the acorn whence it rose. ... I have then lived a long time." Springs, the ancient places of Celtic worship, are the favourite haunts of korrigans, where they sit and comb their long flowing hair. They can assume any form they wish, moving from place to place as quick as thought. Said to cure illnesses by the aid of secret medicines, they rarely let themselves be seen by day. When seen at night, their beauty is great, and their only dress a long white veil which they wrap around their bodies.

Green Willow

"I find it a very difficult wondertale in its form," Alice Kane says. "But it ends the way it has to. There is no other way it can end. The experience jumps up on the hero: he doesn't really have a decision-making hand; he could never have made a decision to take the dis-honourable path. And yet it is a real fairy tale."

The story was translated into English by Grace James and was published in 1910, then again in a revised edition in 1926, as one of the many gift books illustrated, during the golden age of story books, by Warwick Goble. This beautiful book is called *Green Willow, and Other Japanese Fairy Tales*.

The Golden Fly

The wondertales of Ireland remember their beginnings in myth, or stories about the gods, and they remember the gods so well that it is often hard to know where myth ends and wondertale commences. In this fairy tale of a little golden fly who is under a spell, the ancient Celtic gods appear as the Deathless Ones, with Midyir, one of the immortals, promising to make a world for Ethaun, and Ethaun re-plying, in the language of myth: "In all the worlds I would only be a little golden fly, for I have never made a world for myself."

It is a very old story. Known as "The Wooing of Étaín," it is men-tioned in the ancient lists as one of the Prime Stories, and was told as a mythological foretale to the saga of the great King Conaire. The story survives in a 12th-century manuscript called *The Book of the Dun Cow* and, with two other tales of Midyir and Étaín, in *The Yellow Book of Lecan*, a 14th-century manuscript.

The source of Alice Kane's telling is a literary wondertale written by her countrywoman Ella Young (1867–1956) in *Celtic Wonder Tales*, (1910, reissued 1985). This book became very popular in its day, partly for its illustrations contributed by the Irish nationalist and feminist, Maud Gonne MacBride (1866–1953). Miss Kane is deeply grateful to the late Jane Redmond Thompson for many generosities to her over the years, including permission to publish this retelling.

The Peach-Blossom Forest

This story was originally an essay written by the poet Tao Yuanming (Tao Qian, 365–427). Tao lived in a period of corruption, disunity and despair. Finding his intended career of public office bearable only for brief periods, he spent most of his life in retirement in the countryside, where he farmed, studied the Tao, and wrote poetry. This piece, which depicts a Taoist utopia with Taoist goddesses – though in Alice Kane's version their names are the sort that would have been given to bondmaids – is one of the works that every educated Chinese used to read when being trained in literature. The simple statement of a longing for sanity and sanctuary carried two-thousand-year-old memories of the peach tree that stands in Chinese myth as the doorway to the spirit world. To this day, the gift of peaches expresses a wish for a long life.

The retelling is adapted with small changes suggested by the storyteller Kate Stevens from Jo Manton and Robert Gittings, *The Peach-Blossom Forest and Other Chinese Legends*, illustrated by Margery Gill (1951), republished in 1977 as *The Flying Horses: Tales from China*, illustrated by Derek Collard. Alice Kane gratefully acknowledges permission to retell the story, especially the little verse at the end which she found in the 1951 edition. "The book came out during the paper-saving days following the Second War in a very small book," Alice remembers. "But it had the sort of flowery cover of the John Newbery books of long ago. And I loved particularly 'The Peach-Blossom Forest,' and the verse which I have put at the end of the story. I never saw the book in print again. Then there suddenly appeared a book called *The Flying Horses*, and it contained all the stories I remembered from the 1951 edition plus others, but not the little verse: 'Someday, fishing for the thousandth time...'."

The Good Wife

"There was, there was, and yet there was not": so begin these *Yes and No Stories* of the Georgian Republic. It means that what comes after is true, but then again not so true. The storyteller's introduction suits the wisdom, humour and magic of men and women in a bewildering world. The stories were collected by George and Helen Papashvily in *Yes and No Stories: A Book of Georgian Folk Tales*, illustrated by Simon Lissim (1946). Acknowledgment is made to Helen Waite Papashvily for the use of this story.

The Clever Wife

A tale from the mountains and plains of the Kirghiz country, this story was published by Mirra Ginsburg in *The Kaha Bird: Tales from the Steppes of Central Asia*, drawings by Richard Cuffari (1971). Ginsburg's translation evokes the language and ancient wisdom of a semi-nomadic tribal people accustomed to distance and space and to the meeting of East and West, khans and kings, in the crossroads of civilizations. "The Clever Wife" is a useful piece for modern storytelling. It can be told to children, who love its riddles, and, at the same time, to adults, who enjoy the husband-and-wife relationship and the details of social life in the Central Asian kingdoms.

We thank Mirra Ginsburg for her kindness in letting Alice Kane tell this story.

The Lazy Barber's Wife

This is a popular tale from the Punjab, originally the land through which five waters flow in northwest India, before they join the Indus. There, a century ago, Flora Annie Steel (1847–1929) went from village to village in the districts where her husband was a magistrate, collecting the stories that became *Tales of the Punjab: Folklore of India* (1894, reissued 1983). Many familiar kinds of tales are in that book.

While the settings and customs are mysterious to the western European storytelling traditions (except for *The One Thousand and One Nights*, where so many northern Indian stories ended up), one finds in Steel the repetitive nursery tale, the burlesque tale, the trickster tale, and the romance. Like her *English Fairy Tales* (1918), Mrs Steel's collection is full of humour, sturdy characters, and easily remembered rhymes and situations.

The original edition of *Tales of the Punjab* was illustrated by J. Lockwood Kipling (1837–1911), the father of Rudyard Kipling.

The Blue Faience Hippopotamus

The story is adapted from *The Scarlet Fish, and Other Stories* (1942) by Joan Marshall Grant (1907–   ), illustrated by Ralph Lavers. Alice Kane says, "About a generation ago, Joan Grant's historical fiction about Egypt was very popular with both older children and adults. This little collection of fairy tales was much loved, but because perhaps of the greater attraction of the familiar stories of western Europe, especially those of Andersen, which it resembles in many ways, the book was less well known. After the passage of many years, one tale stands out from all the rest: this story of the steadfast, little blue hippopotamus and his love for a human princess. Children and grown-ups both like it, but in very different ways."

The Silver Saucer and the Transparent Apple

As the nineteenth century turned into the twentieth, English-speaking children, who heretofore had known Grimm and Perrault and Andersen, were suddenly introduced to the rich colours of the Russian ballet and also the *skazki*. Authors like Arthur Ransome, Post Wheeler and Ida Zeitlin brought into English the tales of Baba Yaga, the mighty bogatírs, talking swans, firebirds and tsars. Among the best of the wondertales originally collected by Aleksandr Afanas'ev is "The Story of the Silver Saucer and the Crystal Apple."

There are several different retellings for children. However, the enduring version of this wondertale, and the one Alice Kane used as the basis for her storytelling over fifty years ago, is the translation by the English children's book writer and journalist Arthur Ransome (1884–1967) in his *Old Peter's Russian Tales*, illustrated by Dmitri Isidorovich Mitrokhin (1916).

We acknowledge the kindness of John Bell and Rupert Hart-Davis for allowing this story to have a place in the collection.

Childe Rowland

Among the rich variety of British fairy tales, many favourites tell of the rescue of a child or other family member from the enchantment of Faërie. For Alice Kane, this tale brings back those stories, together with the familiar childhood words and magic of tales like "Saint George and the Dragon" and "Jack and the Beanstalk." It recalls landscapes familiar from childhood as well, with some of the superstitions and taboos associated with them. "Those hills with the great winding terraces: they were fortifications of the early British peoples. The entrance to Fairyland was in them. And *widdershins* means going counterclockwise, against the sun — something you should never do, for then your shadow is cast behind you. It says so in the story. But some things you must do widdershins; when you get into Elfland, you see, you have to go widdershins."

The retelling is based on Flora Annie Steel, *English Fairy Tales*, illustrated by Arthur Rackham (1918, reissued 1962).

Tattercoats

Here is an English version of the universal tale of the prince who loves a beggarmaid, perceiving in the charm of a gooseherd's music not her bare feet and her rags but the loveliness of her face and nature. The story can be found in Flora Annie Steel, *English Fairy Tales*.

The Girl Who Took a Snake for a Husband

This Albanian story is a form of the Cupid and Psyche myth — but it is wilder. Hitting your future husband with a ball thrown from a rooftop; finding a house without doors and windows where the old witch crawls out of the roof like a bat; discovering that the spotted snake in the peasant's cart is really a prince; hearing the mountains open and close at noon like thunder: these are the images through which myth becomes folktale in the imagination of a proud mountain people. Their stories come from many sources — some from across the Greek border, and some, in the early days, from China. The retelling is based on a translation by the American writer and diplomat Post Wheeler (1869–1956) found in his *Albanian Wonder Tales* (1936).

Acknowledgments

"Ivon Tortik," from *Three and the Moon: Legendary Stories of Old Brittany, Normandy and Provence* by Jacques Dorey (Alfred A. Knopf, 1929). Used by permission of Random House/Knopf.

"Tsar Saltan and Prince Guidon," from *Skazki: Tales and Legends of Old Russia* by Ida Zeitlin (Doran, 1926).

"The Golden Apples of Lough Erne," translated by Nicholas O'Kearney from the original Irish of the storyteller Abraham M'Coy, published in the *Cambrian Journal* (1855) and collected in *Fairy Tales and Folk Tales of the Irish Peasantry* (1888) by W. B. Yeats.

"The Woman of the Sea," from *The Princess Splendour and Other Stories* by Helen Waddell, (Faber and Faber, 1955), copyright © 1955 the estate of Helen Waddell. Used by permission of Mary M. Martin.

"The Seven Wild Geese" ("The Unique Tale"), from *The King of Ireland's Son* by Pádraic Colum (George C. Harrap, 1920). Copyright © the estate of Pádraic Colum. Used by permission of Máire Colum O'Sullivan.

"The Korrigan," from *French Legends, Tales and Fairy Stories* by Barbara Leonie Picard. Copyright © 1955 by Barbara Leonie Picard. Copyright renewed 1994 by Barbara Leonie Picard. Used by permission of the author.

"Green Willow," from *Green Willow, and Other Japanese Fairy Tales* by Grace James (1910; Macmillan, 1926).

"The Golden Fly," from *Celtic Wonder Tales* by Ella Young (Maunsel, 1910, reissued Floris Books, 1985). Copyright © the estate of Ella Young. Used by permission of Jane Redmond Thompson and the Save the Redwoods League, San Francisco.

"The Peach-Blossom Forest," from *The Peach-Blossom Forest and Other Chinese Legends* by Jo Manton and Robert Gittings. Copyright © 1951 by Jo Manton and Robert Gittings. Copyright renewed 1971 by Jo Manton and Robert Gittings. Used by permission of the authors.

"The Good Wife" ("The Man who had a Good Wife"), from *Yes and No Stories: A Book of Georgian Folk Tales* by George Papashvily and Helen Waite Papashvily. Copyright © 1946 by George Papashvily and Helen Waite Papashvily. Copyright renewed 1974 by George Papashvily and Helen Waite Papashvily. Used by permission of HarperCollins Publishers, Inc.

"The Clever Wife," from *The Kaha Bird: Tales from the Steppes of Central Asia* by Mirra Ginsburg. Copyright © 1971 by Mirra Ginsburg. Used by permission of the author.

"The Lazy Barber's Wife" ("The Barber's Clever Wife"), from *Tales of the Punjab* by Flora Annie Steel (Macmillan, 1894).

"The Blue Faience Hippopotamus," from *The Scarlet Fish, and Other Stories* by Joan Grant. Copyright © 1942 by Joan Grant. Used by permission of A.P. Watt Ltd.

"The Silver Saucer and the Transparent Apple," from *Old Peter's Russian Tales* by Arthur Ransome (1916; Jonathan Cape, 1971), copyright © 1971 the estate of Arthur Ransome. Used by permission of John Bell and Sir Rupert Hart-Davis.

"Childe Rowland" and "Tattercoats," from *English Fairy Tales* by Flora Annie Steel. Copyright © 1918 Macmillan Publishing Company. Copyright renewed 1946 by Mabel H. Webster. Used by permission of Macmillan Books for Young Readers, an imprint of Simon & Schuster Children's Publishing Division.

"The Girl Who Took a Snake for a Husband," from *Albanian Wonder Tales* by Post Wheeler. Copyright © 1936 by Post Wheeler. Used by permission of Doubleday, a division of Bantam Doubleday Dell Publishing Group, Inc.

The author and publisher of this collection have made every reasonable effort to contact copyright holders. Should there be a property that remains to be settled, we will be glad to have the matter brought to our attention.

This book was designed by Robert Bringhurst, set into type by Susanne Gilbert at the Typeworks, Vancouver, and printed and bound by Tim Inkster at the Porcupine's Quill in Erin, Ontario.

Monotype Centaur is the text face. It is based on a design created in 1912–14 by Bruce Rogers, which was itself a revision – a typographic *retelling*, so to speak – of a font cut in Venice in 1468 by Nicolas Jenson. Jenson's font was likewise a retelling in metal of an alphabet developed by Venetian scribes from 8th-century Carolingian models. These trace their ancestry in turn through Irish uncials to Roman and Greek scripts and on to still earlier sources in the eastern Mediterranean.

Centaur's companion italic – Monotype Arrighi – is derived from the designs of Frederic Warde, which are founded on those of the 16th-century Roman calligrapher Ludovico degli Arrighi. Behind Arrighi's letterforms stand the same Italian, Irish and Mediterranean sources that nourish Centaur roman.

The title and large initials in this book are set in Carol Twombly's Charlemagne, which is based directly on Carolingian manuscript capitals likewise steeped in the Irish scribal tradition.

The rooster emblem owes its form to Russian folk art. Its immediate precursor is a woodcut made by Theodore Nadejan for Ida Zeitlin's *Skazki: Tales and Legends of Old Russia* (New York: Doran, 1926).

The frontispiece photograph of Alice Kane was made by Ben Mark Holzberg for the Storytellers School of Toronto.

ALICE KANE was born in Ireland in 1908. Moving with her parents to Canada in 1921, she was educated in New Brunswick and at McGill University in Montreal before beginning a career with the Toronto Public Library, where she had a major interest in fairy tales. After her retirement in 1973, she taught Children's Literature at the University of New Brunswick, then began a second career as a professional storyteller in association with the Storytellers School of Toronto. She has been a featured performer at many storytelling events, including the American Storytelling Festival at Jonesborough, Tennessee. Her rich oral heritage is remembered in *Songs and Sayings of an Ulster Childhood*, edited by Edith Fowke (1983).

SEAN KANE — Alice Kane's nephew and a long-time listener to her wondertales — is Professor of English and Cultural Studies at Trent University, near Toronto. He is the author of *Spenser's Moral Allegory* (1989), *Wisdom of the Mythtellers* (1994), and, with Kelly Liberty, *Nursery Rhymes for Colicky Parents*, illustrated by Gillian Johnson (1995).